IMAGES of America
RESIDENTS OF OAKLAND CEMETERY

Map of Atlanta. Mapmakers Saunders and Kline's 1892 "Bird Eye View" map of Atlanta gives a detailed perspective of how the city was developing. The map is cropped here to give a closer look at Oakland and how it was laid out. By now, the City of Atlanta had purchased all of the 48 acres the cemetery now occupies. The complete bird's-eye view map is at the Library of Congress. (Library of Congress.)

On the Cover: Burial Grounds. This photograph shows the burial grounds directly behind Oakland's Bell Tower. Taken in 1984, it reflects the efforts the Historic Oakland Foundation made towards reclaiming overgrown areas of the neglected cemetery. Merchant and newspaperman Edwin W. Marsh's mausoleum is on the right. The Gatlin family, whose graves are in the foreground, were the original owners of the Georgian Terrace Hotel. (Historic Oakland Foundation.)

IMAGES of America
RESIDENTS OF OAKLAND CEMETERY

Janice McDonald

Copyright © 2019 by Janice McDonald
ISBN 978-1-4671-0398-5

Published by Arcadia Publishing
Charleston, South Carolina

Library of Congress Control Number: 2019937268

For all general information, please contact Arcadia Publishing:
Telephone 843-853-2070
Fax 843-853-0044
E-mail sales@arcadiapublishing.com
For customer service and orders:
Toll-Free 1-888-313-2665

Visit us on the Internet at www.arcadiapublishing.com

I would like to dedicate this book to the employees, volunteers, and members of the Historic Oakland Foundation, who have worked hard and continue to do so to help preserve Oakland, its grounds, and its incredible history.

Contents

Acknowledgments		6
Introduction		7
1.	The Atlanta Cemetery	9
2.	Bell Tower Ridge and Surrounding Areas	35
3.	African American Grounds	73
4.	Jewish Grounds	91
5.	Confederate Memorial Grounds	107
6.	East Hill	115

Acknowledgments

This book could not have happened without the support of so many friends, family, and even strangers (now new friends). The staff and volunteers at the Historic Oakland Foundation opened their doors and readily imparted their knowledge to help me tell the tales of these residents. First, I would like to thank director David Moore, who signed off on my idea, and Visitors Center and gift shop manager Tim Wright, who introduced me to so many people. Marcy Breffle, Oakland's education manager, is a font of knowledge and tolerated my constant questions. Sara VanBeck spent so much time helping me on my information hunts and gave me context to Oakland's past. Ashley Shares, Jennifer Chisholm, and Angie Wynne also were so quick to respond. D.L. Henderson's passion for history is so evident, as is her knowledge of those in the African American Grounds. I cannot even count the numerous volunteers who helped me look through the burial books to find locations of residents I was searching for. Linda Feree, Sharon Doyle, Ruth Middleton, and Oakland Sexton Sam Reed were last-minute angels.

Those outside of Oakland itself were also eager to help, especially when it came to sharing stories of their ancestors. So many Oakland residents are connected to one another! A big thanks goes to David and Leslye Hardie, Barbara Regenstein, Beth Puglisi, Kelly Stocks, and Barb Parks for their help and enthusiasm in sharing their families' stories. Judith Anderson Vanderver uncovered long-hidden photographs of the funerals of Gov. John E. Brown and his wife, Elizabeth. Davie Lemer Davis and I spent hours poring through her family's history.

I am forever grateful to the researchers who helped with the digging, including Jena Jones and Paul Crater from the Atlanta History Center, Kirk Henderson and Tom Fisher from Georgia Tech, Jeremy Katz from the Breman Museum, Alison Hudgins of the Georgia State Archives, Leigh Reynolds of the Atlanta Women's Club, Barbara Kievit-Mason at Sam Houston State University, and Billy Wade of the National Archives.

Finally, I want to thank Jeff Ruetsche at Arcadia, who helped get the ball rolling, and my title manager Caroline Anderson, who kept me on task and carried it over the line.

Because there are many of the photographs that I received from the same sources, I have abbreviated in some cases. The Library of Congress is LOC. Historic Oakland Foundation is HOF. Atlanta History Center is AHC.

Introduction

Inside the brick walls that surround Oakland Cemetery, you will find an unexpected sanctuary of history, peace, and beauty. It is as much a garden as it is a place where people have been laid to rest. Ancient brick pathways connect landscaped plots adorned with statuary and ornately carved tombstones. Inscriptions both poetic and telling can trigger the imagination. You will want to come back, as I have, time and time again—always discovering something new. I drove by those walls hundreds of times before I finally ventured in and now, I can't stay away. Many of the prominent family names of Atlanta can be seen here on headstones and mausoleums along with those of the lesser known people who helped shape the city. Wandering through Oakland and reading those names is like being on a historical treasure hunt.

Oakland had its beginnings not long after Atlanta established itself as a bustling and growing metropolis. The town, originally called Terminus, was the product of a confluence of railroads. As the rail system grew, so did the community; and as time goes on, so do life and the inevitable. Atlanta needed a place to bury its dead.

The city purchased six acres of land in 1850, in what was considered the countryside on the outskirts of town, from A.W. Wooding. Wooding's wife, Agnes, had just passed away and had been buried on the very property that he sold.

It became very apparent soon enough that six acres wouldn't meet Atlanta's needs. The growing Jewish population of the city petitioned for their own burial area. A place was needed to bury the African American slaves. Looking to the future, more land was needed. Within five years, 15 more acres were purchased and then more, until it became the 48 acres it is today.

But that growth did not come without controversy. Two years after this became a public cemetery, the city granted permission to bury African Americans in a segregated area in the back part of the original six acres. It was named Slave Square, although not all of the African Americans buried there were slaves. But as the cemetery grew and more plots were sold, Slave Square was becoming surrounded by whites and the square became coveted territory.

In 1866, land located in the farthest reaches of the cemetery was designated as the new segregated African American burial ground, and in 1877, the more than 800 people buried in the Slave Square were dug up and buried in the "colored pauper grounds." The square was replotted and sold to whites.

The Civil War also created changes at Oakland. Many of the largest Confederate hospitals were located in Atlanta, so the wounded were brought here. A section at the heart of the cemetery was set aside to become the Confederate Memorial Grounds. Battles got closer and closer until, during the Battle of Atlanta, the fighting raged virtually just outside the cemetery's gates. There was a farmhouse where the Bell Tower now stands, and Gen. John Bell Hood watched the fighting progress from that high vantage point.

More than 7,000 Confederates and 16 Union soldiers are now buried here, including 3,000 who are buried as unknowns. The cemetery records also list boxes of limbs being buried.

Atlanta City Cemetery was official renamed Oakland Cemetery in 1876 to honor the numerous oak trees growing on its grounds. What had been farmland was taking on more of a garden atmosphere as the families of those buried here were honoring their dead with elaborate headstones and landscaping. The noble arched entrance of the Hunter Street gate was erected in 1896, and four years later, the Bell Tower was completed.

While Oakland is a cemetery, it was also a business owned by the City of Atlanta. Plots were purchased through the city. The deeds were originally signed by the mayor and the city clerk. The cemetery's popularity also meant business for marble and granite dealers who prided themselves on their creations. Families wanted theirs to stand out. Some of most humble in life were celebrated in death, while many of Atlanta's larger names chose more unassuming markers. The heaviest of monuments were off-loaded from the neighboring railroad and brought into the grounds.

By the late 1880s, all of Oakland's plots had been sold and with that went the city's ability to make money off the cemetery. With little money coming in, the cemetery became almost an afterthought. It had always been up to the families to maintain their own gravesites; as time passed, the families themselves were dying off or descendants felt little connection to their long-ago ancestors.

Oakland was itself a dying cemetery when a group of Atlantans chose to save it in the 1970s by forming the non-profit Historic Oakland Foundation. The cemetery was added to the National Register of Historic Places in 1976, and that helped launch concerted efforts to restore it and thoroughly document its history and its people.

Through grants, donations, special events, and sheer willpower, HOF continues to work to bring Oakland back to its former glory. The foundation is never done on its restoration efforts, and the work to maintain the grounds is ongoing. While there is a small staff, the foundation relies heavily on the work of volunteers, who do everything from helping with tours and manning the gift shop to working with landscaping and plants to researching the history of Oakland itself. Efforts to undo decades of neglect have helped reclaim graves choked by weeds, repair collapsed tombstones, and, in some cases, create new monuments for those residents who were unmarked or whose marker had disintegrated.

These 48 acres are now home to about 70,000 residents, with a few dozen still added each year. This book is an effort to highlight some of the known, some of the lesser known, and some of the forgotten. There are 27 former Atlanta mayors here as well as six former governors. *Gone with the Wind* author Margaret Mitchell and acclaimed golfer Bobby Jones also rest here. Their stories are known, so I have chosen to try and mix the mostly unrecognized in with a few of the names you may know.

The cemetery itself is divided into sections, and I have noted where the residents I have profiled are buried in case you want to visit them yourselves. The original six acres are on either side of the main road as you come through the Hunter Street gate. Bell Tower Ridge is where the cemetery offices and gift shop are located. That chapter includes the sections which surround it, including areas some call Knit Hill, Hogpen Corner, and Greenhouse Valley. The African American section, Jewish section, and the area called East Hill lie farther from the gate but have so many incredible residents to visit. The Confederate Memorial Grounds are well defined, but the residents are less so. I have picked just a handful of graves as a representation of some of the stories of the men who lie here.

There are countless more stories that could be told. I hope that telling these will make you want to seek them out on your own.

One

The Atlanta Cemetery

Agnes Harriet Wooding (D. 1850). Agnes Harriet Wooding (Section 9, Block 459) was buried on her family's property outside Atlanta when she died in 1850. A month later, her husband sold the land to for the city to use as the Atlanta City Cemetery, making her unofficially Oakland's first resident. When her husband died 28 years later, he was buried next to her. Her tombstone bears the image of a weeping willow. (Janice McDonald.)

Dr. James Nissen (d. 1850). The first person to officially be buried in the new Atlanta Cemetery was not an Atlanta resident. Dr. James Nissen (Section 1) fell ill while visiting in the fall of 1850, soon after land for the new Atlanta Cemetery was purchased. Fearing being buried alive, Nissen made friend and fellow surgeon Dr. Charles d'Alvigney promise to cut his jugular vein after he died to ensure his death. D'Alvigney upheld his vow in front of horrified witnesses just prior to Nissen being interred. (Janice McDonald.

Martha Lumpkin Compton (1827–1917). Martha Lumpkin (Section 1 Public grounds) was only 16 when her father, Georgia governor William Lumpkin, renamed a growing town of Terminus "Marthasville" after her. Some residents felt the name was not grand enough. The name "Atlantica-Pacifica" was suggested instead. That name was shortened to "Atlanta" and adopted in 1845. Oddly enough, Martha's full name was Martha Atalanta Wilson Lumpkin. (AHC.)

Gen. James Birdseye McPherson (1823–1864). A career military man, Gen. James McPherson (Section 1, Block 55) was a captain stationed in California when the Civil War began. He requested a transfer east and quickly began rising through the ranks. Brig. Gen. Ulysses S. Grant himself recommended his promotion to general. The second-highest-ranking Union officer to die during the war, McPherson was shot and killed in the early days of the Battle of Atlanta. (LOC.)

Thomas G.W. Crusselle (1822 –1890). Thomas Crusselle (Section 1, Lot 134) was a well-known contractor in Atlanta and credited for building the celebrated Calico house downtown. Crusselle was part of the Atlanta Surrender party, which included Julius Hayden, William Markham, Alfred Austell, E.E. Rawson, J.E. Williams, and Thomas Kile. The black unionist Robert Webster rode along with the white men to present the city to Gen. William Tecumseh Sherman. (Janice McDonald.)

SARAH TODD IVY (1782–1865). Sarah Ivy (Section 1, Lot 158) and her husband, Hardy (1779–1842), were the first known settlers of European decent to move to the area that would eventually become Atlanta. They purchased 202.5 acres of lot 51, or the 14th district of then Dekalb County, in what had been Creek Indian territory. Moving from their native South Carolina, they built a log cabin in the wilderness three years before the area was surveyed to lay railroad tracks. The Ivys had 13 children before Hardy died after falling from a horse. It is unclear where he is buried. The location of their cabin was near what is now the corner of Ellis and Courtland Streets. This artist's depiction of the Ivy cabin is found at the Atlanta History Center. (AHC.)

Capt. John T. Milledge (1837–1898). As the son of a governor and the namesake of the town of Milledgeville, Capt. John T. Milledge (Section 1, Lot 22) felt called to serve. He attended the Georgia Military Institute and served in the First Georgia Regulars during the Civil War. Post-conflict, Milledge opened a law office in Atlanta, helped to procure funds for Grady Hospital, and was elected state librarian. Milledge established the Governor's Horse Guard and helped organize the Fulton County Veterans Association. (*Memoirs of Georgia.*)

Fanny Milledge (1844–1895). Fanny Milledge (Section 1, Lot 22) championed her husband's love of the Confederacy and became head of the Ladies' Memorial Association. She led the push to place marble headstones on the graves of the Confederate soldiers at Oakland Cemetery. She also commissioned the Lion of Atlanta monument honoring the unknown Confederate dead. Mrs. Milledge personally unveiled it at the dedication. She died one year later. (*Memoirs of Georgia.*)

DIDERICK AUGUST DOMINI (1855–1886). D.A. Domini (Section 1, Block 39) was born in the Lower Saxony region of Germany. He and his older brother John (1849–1907) moved to the United States after the Civil War. John opened a saloon that advertised "good food," even serving "fresh Mobile oysters" from time to time at 60¢ a dozen. Diderick was very active in the Odd Fellows fraternal organization, which helped erect his monument at Oakland. (Janice McDonald.)

DR. BENJAMIN O. JONES (1801–1867). Dr. B.O. Jones (Section 1, Lot 71) was one of the earliest settlers in the booming new town of Atlanta. He came to the city from his plantation in Fayette County in about 1850 and soon established himself as a city leader. A member of the Know-Nothing Party, he became involved in helping organize infrastructure of the new town and was among those who helped charter the Atlanta Bank in 1852. (Janice McDonald.)

CARRIE MABRY BERRY CRUMLEY (1854–1921).
Carrie Crumley (Section 1, Block 410) turned 10 years old while Atlanta was under siege. During the Civil War, she chronicled her day-to-day life between 1864 and 1866 in a diary, recounting everything from the constant barrage of shells to food shortages. The recollections were later published as *A Confederate Girl: The Diary of Carrie Berry*. Her own son William Gregg Crumley (1885–1924) later served in World War I. (AHC.)

GEORGE WASHINGTON JACK (1840–1904).
Like his brothers, G.W. Jack (Section 2, Block 332) was a wholesaler dealer of candies and crackers. A newspaper article described the business: "The commodious and well-filled confectionery of G.W. Jack on Whitehall Street may be well called one of the institutions of Atlanta." One year's sales at G.W. Jacks were $150,000. Jack was also known for his generosity in giving candy gifts to school children. (*Atlanta Daily Herald*.)

COMMISSION MERCHANTS.
WHITEHALL ST.
ATLANTA, GA.

Dec. 26, 1868—3m.

G. W. JACK & CO.

 STEAM **CANDY**

AND

 CRACKER MANUFACTORY,

AND DEALERS IN

 TOYS  TOYS TOYS TOYS

WILLOW WARE,

And everything kept in a first class Confectionery.

Dec. 19—3m.   **Whitehall Street,**..........................**ATLANTA GA.**

Murdered Her Two Sisters.

Miss Julia Force, sister of the leading shoe merchant of Atlanta, Ga., shot and killed her two sisters. The shooting was the result of a family quarrel. They all moved in the highest social circles. The woman says that she has been writing for a year on a statement of the family troubles and has just completed it. As the proper time to do the deed she chose a day when her mother was absent from the house, she sent the servants out on errands, and then, going to the room where her sister Florence was sick in bed, she placed a pistol to her right temple and shot her dead. Then going to the kitchen, where her other sister was, she shot her in the same manner. Miss Force calmly locked the door and went to the police station. The bodies of the women were found by a brother, to whom she had sent a message to the effect that her sister Florence was worse. In response he went home to find the bodies of his dead sisters.

FLORENCE FORCE (1861–1893) AND MINNIE FORCE (1865–1893). Florence and Minnie Force's (Section 2, Block 250) graves are unmarked to prevent curiosity-seekers. Claiming they had mistreated her, older sister Julia murdered her sisters while their brothers were at the family shoe store. She was found innocent by reason of insanity and died in the state mental hospital. Newspapers across the globe carried gruesome details of the murder and the trial. (*Birmingham Eccentric Newspaper*, March 1893.)

OSWALD HOUSTON (1798–1861). Oswald Houston (Section 2, Block 75) was Atlanta's first city treasurer and served in the position for numerous terms. He moved from his native South Carolina just as Atlanta was in its infancy. Houston helped found Atlanta's First Sunday school. Although it was originally ecumenical, he was instrumental in helping form what is now the First Presbyterian Church of Atlanta. (Janice McDonald.)

JASPER NEWTON SMITH (1833–1919). Jasper Smith (Section 1, Lot 66) wore many hats: farmer, contractor, brick manufacturer, and proprietor of the Bachelors Domain Hotel. One thing he wouldn't wear was a necktie. When his statue was created for his mausoleum, the sculptor gave it a necktie. Smith refused payment until it was removed. He built his fortune largely selling bricks for the rebuilding of Atlanta. His mausoleum is built of rejected granite paving bricks that had been meant for Atlanta streets. Smith's office building stood on the site of what is now the Five Points MARTA station. A marble slab pays tribute to the unusual structure and bears the words "the House that Jack built." (Above, *The Cotton States and International Exhibition South Illustrated*; below, Janice McDonald.)

Joseph Winship (1800–1878). Joseph Winship (Section 8, Lot 271) apprenticed as a shoe and boot maker in his home state of Massachusetts, and when his employer moved south he followed. Joe and his brother Isaac build a tannery in Forsyth, Georgia. Joe sold out to Isaac, opened a cotton gin, and eventually moved to Atlanta to start building and repairing railroad cars. He was so busy that he built his own foundry next to the rail yard to keep up with the demands. Foundry Street was named for the Winship Machine Company. Joe eventually turned operations of the company over to his sons Robert and George, who, during the war, helped operate it to support the Confederacy. Union soldiers dismantled the foundry during the occupation of Atlanta. The Winships rebuilt it and operated it for many years. (Both, AHC.)

MARCUS ARELLEUS BELL (1828–1885). Attorney Marcus Bell (Section 8, Lot 272) was known as owner of "the Calico House." The building was constructed of plaster-covered stone and marbleized in various shades of blue, yellow, and red. Atlantans commented that the exterior looked like calico fabric. Gen. William T. Sherman's engineering corps occupied the house during the Civil War. Years later, the home became Wesley Memorial Hospital, the precursor to Emory University Hospital. (*City Builder Magazine*.)

ORELIA KEY BELL (1864–1959). Orelia Bell grew up in the Calico House and gained international acclaim as a poet. Her most famous works are a series of hymns for the Christian Science Church. Orelia listed her inspiration as Ida Jane Ash. Ash was her companion for more than 50 years, and she penned her poem "Ida Ash" in her honor. The two are buried beside one another in Section 8, Lot 273. (*Poems of Orelia Key Bell.*)

JAMES CRAWFORD FREEMAN (1819–1885). Raised on a Jones County plantation, James Freeman (Section 6, Block 329) had a privileged upbringing. His family owned almost 90 slaves, yet he opposed secession. Still, Freeman served as a lieutenant colonel in the Confederate army. Afterwards, Freeman was elected to Congress as a Republican and notably appointed Henry Ossian Flipper to West Point. Flipper became the first black graduate of the US Military Academy. (LOC.)

THOMAS SHIVER (1817–1862). Thomas Shivers (Section 9, Block 561) came to Terminus as a stagecoach driver. While serving as deputy marshal, he was challenged for the office by colorful Civil War veteran Capt. G. Whit Anderson. Animus between them lead to a pistol duel on Whitehall Street. Shivers was killed in the first recorded death of a law officer in Atlanta. Anderson was acquitted and later became a police officer. (Janice McDonald.)

SARAH KUGLAR DYE (1828–1888). When Sarah Dye's (Section 8, Lot 428) husband, Thomas (1816–1890), went off to fight at Big Shanty, she hid with her three children in makeshift bunkers to avoid possible shelling with the invasion of Atlanta expected. Her youngest son, John Morgan (1862–1864), became ill, and she was unable to get him proper treatment. He died just as the shelling of Atlanta began. Family stories recount that the distraught mother put his body in a box and walked to Oakland to bury him by herself. Along the way, she met a slave with a wagon, who helped her dig John Morgan's grave—using mostly their hands. She then implored the man to save himself and slept on her son's grave before returning to her other children. John Morgan's grave is in the foreground, with Sarah's to the left. (Janice McDonald.)

S. B. OATMAN,
MARBLE DEALER.

MONUMENTS,

TOMBS,

HEAD-STONES,

MANTELS,

VASES,

Furnishing Marble.

South of the Georgia Railroad Depot, Atlanta, Georgia.

STEPHEN B. OATMAN (1815–1903). Advertisements for the marble company owned by Stephen B. Oatman (Section 8, Lot 252) listed him as dealing in "Italian, American and Egyptian Marble." Everything from tombs and statues to furnishings, Oatman's works mark many of the graves at Oakland. The company's offices were located near the Georgia Railroad, but Oatman purchased a plantation known as Melora in Powder Springs in 1864. He had not owned it long before the Kennesaw Campaign of the Civil War brought Union soldiers to the plantation. Brig. Gen. Alpheus Williams and several of his subordinates in the First Division of the Twentieth Corps took over the residence as their battle house during the Kolb Farm Battle. (*Southern Confederacy Newspaper.*)

Col. George Washington Harrison (1849–1936). Col. G.W. Harrison (Section 8, Lot 315) was a popular business and civic leader in early Atlanta. A 1906 assessment of outstanding Georgia leaders labeled him "cordial, genial and courteous, a man of integrity and honor." Harrison was head of the Franklin Printing Company, managing numerous publications. During the Civil War, he served as on the military staff of Govs. Willian Northern, William Atkinson, and Joseph Terrill. (*Memoirs of Georgia*.)

Ernest Christian Kontz (1814–1881). German-born Ernest Kontz (Section 8, Lot 289) commissioned this Egyptian-themed memorial as a resting place for himself, his wife, Mary Elizabeth Trabert Kontz (1821–1878), and several of their children. The gate is complete with images of Isis, the goddess of the Nile, and lotus flowers. Kontz was an entrepreneur, involved in farming and horticulture. His home at 80 Marietta Street was one of the first brick homes in Atlanta. (Janice McDonald.)

MARY ELLEN "NELLIE" PETERS BLACK (1851–1919). The *Atlanta Journal* wrote that the name of Nellie Peters Black (Section 9, Block 577) "was a synonym for charity, for gentleness of spirit, for love of humanity, for constructive citizenship." The daughter of railroad man Richard Peters, she married Congressman Georgia Robinson Black (1848–1886), raising his four children as her own. She belonged to numerous civic organizations, including the Georgia Federation of Women's Clubs, where she served as president three times. Devoutly religious, Black organized Atlanta's first health mission, serving on the founding board of the King's Daughters Hospital (the city's first free hospital). Following the death of her husband, she lobbied the legislature to allow women into the University of Georgia. She also spoke at agricultural rallies to promote diversified crops. Shortly before her death, she convinced Atlanta Public Schools to begin including kindergartens. (AHC.)

Harriet Eliza Cone Hayden (1829–1899), Julius Augustus Hayden (1810–1890). Harriet Hayden (Section 8, Lot 304–305) was the matriarch of one of Atlanta's most prominent families. Her husband, Julius Hayden (1810–1890), was a judge, as was her father. Harriet was a small girl when Julius first met her while traveling to Georgia from Connecticut. When she came of age, she joined him in his home state to be married before they both returned to Atlanta. Her son Reuben Cone Hayden (1871–1899) was a well-known businessman and leader of Atlanta society but died at the age of 29 of pneumonia. His unexpected death created numerous problems with unfinished business dealings, including a dispute over a marriage contract between his own grandmother, Lucinda Cone, and Judge W.H. Underwood. (Above, HOF; below, Janice McDonald.)

ALONZO CHASE LADD (1832–1893). Alonzo Ladd (Section 8, Block 338) first came to Atlanta selling lightning rods. He purchased a lime quarry in Bartow County and established the A.C. Lime Company, which traded and manufactured plaster, cement, and lime. Ladd was fascinated with the afterlife, often attending seances, and gave speeches about connecting with the dead. He met his own demise while seeking relief from chronic pain in Las Vegas. (Janice McDonald.)

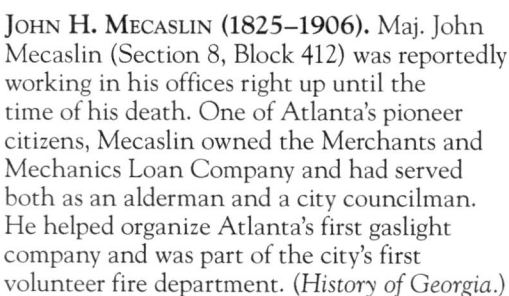

JOHN H. MECASLIN (1825–1906). Maj. John Mecaslin (Section 8, Block 412) was reportedly working in his offices right up until the time of his death. One of Atlanta's pioneer citizens, Mecaslin owned the Merchants and Mechanics Loan Company and had served both as an alderman and a city councilman. He helped organize Atlanta's first gaslight company and was part of the city's first volunteer fire department. (*History of Georgia*.)

FABIAN BROWN (1826–1897). German native Fabian Brown (Section 8, Lot 222) was simply walking in downtown Atlanta when he dropped dead, causing quite a stir. The newspaper lamented that even at age 71, he "seemed to have been in good health" and was a regular figure on the streets. He had amassed a "considerable fortune" through his hard work in several business ventures and his noted frugality. (HOF.)

MARY ELIZABETH NEAL (1867–1889), MARY CASH NEAL (1844–1894). Lizzy Neal and her mother, Mollie Neal (Section 8, Block 349), were immortalized in marble by father and husband Thomas Benton Neal (1832–1908). Lizzy had already lost six siblings from various ailments and was suffering from rheumatism for months before her death while her mother attempted to nurse her. Lizzy is believed to be the figure on the right. (Janice McDonald.)

JOHN NEAL (1796–1886). John "Jack" Neal (Section 8, Block 446–44) built a home known as a showplace, making it a coveted location for Gen. William T. Sherman to use as a home during his occupation of Atlanta. The house was first depicted in *Leslie's Weekly* and then shown again after Sherman left it. A farmer, merchant, and capitalist, Neal was considered the richest man in Atlanta. His fortune could not save him from the tragedy of losing sons Andrew (1837–1864) and James (1835–1865) in the final months of the Civil War. Sherman is said to have watched Atlanta burn while sitting on the balcony of the Neal home. The Neals never moved back to their house, choosing to abandon it. It was used at the Girls' High School for almost 50 years. Atlanta City Hall is now located on the property where it stood. (Above, *Leslie's Weekly*; below, LOC.)

Lt. Andrew Jackson Neal (1837–1864). Although he was from Atlanta, Lt. A.J. Neal (Section 8, Block 446-44) was commissioned into the Marion Light Artillery Regiment while in Amelia Island, Florida, on June 15, 1861. He was quickly promoted to first lieutenant. Neal participated in the Battle of Richmond, Kentucky, and well as the Battle of Chickamauga. He was killed while fighting in his hometown of Atlanta on August 10, 1864. (Janice McDonald.)

Col. James Henry Neal (1835–1865). Col. James Neal (Section 8, Block 446-44) was first commissioned in the Georgia 19th Infantry Regiment on June 11, 1861. Within a year, he was promoted to major, reaching full colonel by August 1863. He was killed in one of the final clashes of the war, falling in the Battle of Bentonville in North Carolina. The arch shape of the headstone he shares with his brother depicts their unity in serving the Confederacy. (Janice McDonald.)

RICHARD PETERS (1810–1889). Richard Peters (Section 9. Block 477) moved from Philadelphia to Marthasville to become the superintendent of the state railroad. He is credited with pushing to change the town's name to Atlanta. Peters established numerous businesses, including Atlanta's first steam-powered cotton mill. To have wood to generate steam, Peters bought 405 acres of forest in what is now Midtown. He later subdivided the land, donating four acres to establish the Georgia School of Technology, now Georgia Tech. (AHC.)

E. JEFFERSON CAIN (1827–1897). Jeff Cain (Section 9, Block 520) was made famous by the "Great Locomotive Chase." He was the engineer of the railroad engine *The General*, which was stolen as part of a Union-backed raid on April 12, 1862. The instigators were called "Andrews Raiders" after civilian scout James T. Andrews, who led them. After seven hours of pursuit, Cain, along with fellow Oakland residents William Fuller and Anthony Murphy, regained control of the locomotive. (AHC.)

OSBORNE AUGUSTUS LOCHRANE (1829–1887). Dubbed "The Irish Orator of Georgia," Judge Osborne Lochrane (Section 9, Block 336) was known for his flowery speech. He wrote the inscription on his ornate Oakland column, which reads, "Land of my adoption where the loved sleep folded in the embrace of your flowers. Would that it were my destiny to increase the flood tide of your glory, as it has been mine to share your fortunes: For when my years tremble to their close, I would sleep beneath your soil where the drip of april tears may fall upon my grave; and the sunshine of your skies warm southern flowers to bloom upon my breast." Lochrane was for a time Gov. John E. Brown's law partner. He served a year as chief justice of the Georgia Supreme Court before resigning to become the attorney for the Pullman Palace Car Company. (Right, AHC; below, Janice McDonald.)

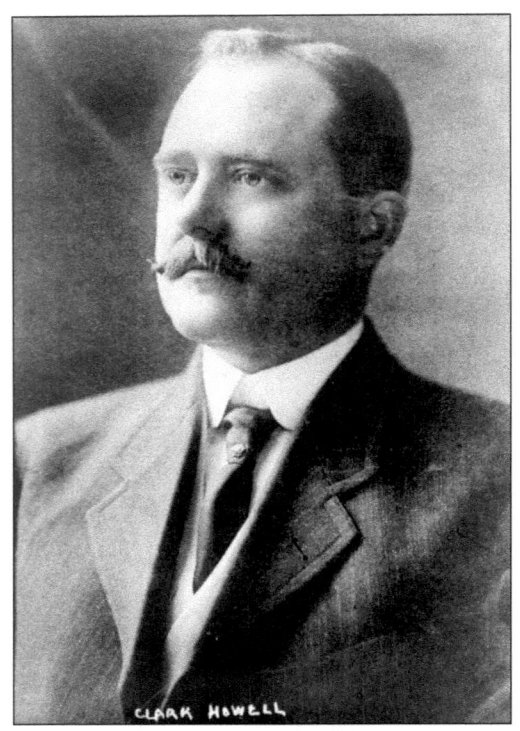

CLARK FORSYTHE HOWELL (1811–1882). Judge Clark Howell (Section 9, Block 584) was a business and landowner in Gwinnett County, moving to Cobb County after the death of his first wife, Martha Ann Wynn (1822–1837), during childbirth. When his second wife, Effiah Jane Park (1817–1850), passed away, he moved to Atlanta, where he became a judge. Howell helped supervise the creation of Fulton County. He also built Howell Mill, for which the street was named. (LOC.)

JACOB J. SCHIKEN (1860–1906). Jacob J. Schiken (Section 9, Lot 577) was the son of immigrants from the Netherlands and established a successful grocery business in Atlanta. When he married Mary Green Schiken (1861–1888) at Saints Peter and Paul Church in 1886, the *Atlanta Constitution* referred to him as one of the city's most promising young businessmen. It also described the new Mrs. Schiken as a "much admired young lady." (Atlanta City Records.)

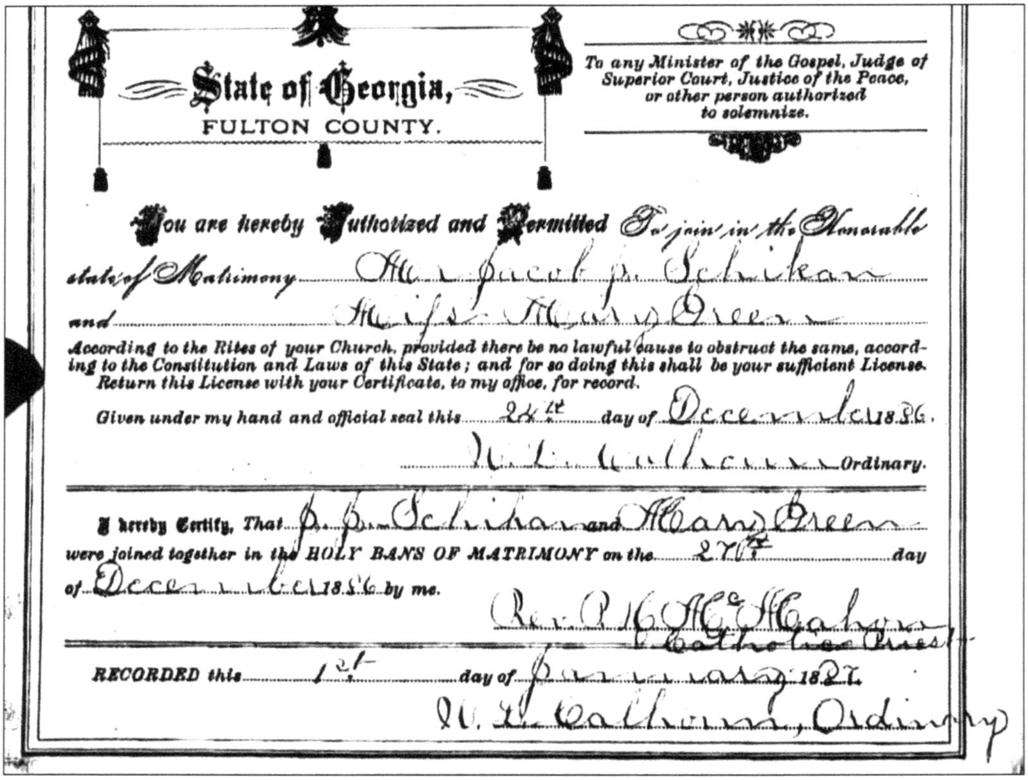

State of Georgia,
FULTON COUNTY.

To any Minister of the Gospel, Judge of Superior Court, Justice of the Peace, or other person authorized to solemnize.

You are hereby Authorized and Permitted To join in the Honorable state of Matrimony Mr. Jacob J. Schiken and Miss Mary Green According to the Rites of your Church, provided there be no lawful cause to obstruct the same, according to the Constitution and Laws of this State; and for so doing this shall be your sufficient License. Return this License with your Certificate, to my office, for record.

Given under my hand and official seal this 24th day of December 1886.

W. L. Calhoun Ordinary.

I hereby Certify, That J. J. Schiken and Mary Green were joined together in the HOLY BANS OF MATRIMONY on the 27th day of December 1886 by me.

Rev. R. K. McMahon
Catholic Priest

RECORDED this 1st day of January 1887.

W. L. Calhoun, Ordinary

WILLIAM JASPER FRANKLIN (1849–1910). William "the Goat Man" Franklin (Section 9, Lot 578) made his way around downtown Atlanta in a cart, pulled by his goat Pete. Paralyzed by meningitis at age 19, Franklin earned money selling pencils or apples to help his blind father and invalid mother. While some considered him a likeable character, many in the legislature considered him a nuisance. They passed a measure to outlaw Franklin's activities around the capital. The law was never enforced. While Franklin was originally buried in an unmarked grave, the Historic Oakland Foundation raised money for a tombstone. He is portrayed here at the dedication of the stone by Oakland volunteer Tom Deardorff. Pictured, from left to right, are Deardorff and David Moore, executive director of Historic Oakland. (James Meeks.)

FRANKLIN MILLER GARRETT (1906–2000). Franklin Garrett (Public Block Grave 3 B) was Atlanta's only official historian. His meticulous research of the city's past was chronicled in his *Atlanta and Environs: A Chronicle of its People and Events*. Originally published in 1987, the book has an attention to detail that makes it still one of the most referred to records on Atlanta history; it was used in the research for this book. Garrett was born in Milwaukee, and he moved to Atlanta as a child. He was Coca-Cola's historian for 28 years. His love for history led him in 1930 to record all of the headstones in Oakland. In retirement, Garrett devoted his time to the Atlanta History Center, including volunteering at Oakland. (Both, AHC.)

Two

Bell Tower Ridge and Surrounding Areas

Mary Isabel Mitchell (1872–1919). "Maybelle" Mitchell (Section 2, Block 22) was an attorney and an activist. She served as head of the Atlanta Woman's Suffrage League in 1915 and later as president of the Atlanta Board of Education. Mitchell was also active in numerous church and literary societies. Her Civil War veteran husband Eugene Muse Mitchell (1866–1944) made his fortune in lumber during the rebuilding of Atlanta. From left to right are Margaret, Maybelle, and Stephen Mitchell. Daughter Margaret penned *Gone with the Wind*. (AHC.)

WILLIAM ALLEN FULLER (1836–1905). William Fuller (Section 3, Block 72) was infamously the conductor of the train pulled by the engine that was captured by Andrews Raiders at Big Shanty in 1862. In what was immortalized as "The Great Locomotive Chase," Captain Fuller joined the train foreman and a group of Confederate soldiers in an 87-mile pursuit; they finally recaptured *The General* just two miles north of Ringgold, Georgia. (LOC.)

ANTHONY MURPHY (1829–1909). Anthony Murphy (Section 3, Block 42) was foreman of Machinery and Motive Power for the Western & Atlantic Railroad in northern Georgia when the Civil War erupted. The infamous "Great Locomotive Chase" involved his engine *The General*. Sounding an alert, Murphy joined conductor William Fuller and chased the locomotive into North Georgia, where it was recaptured. Murphy later served on the Atlanta City Council. (*Memoirs of Georgia*.)

FREDERIC AMMI WILLIAMS (1817–1883) AND MARY J.E. NELSON WILLIAMS (1825–1845). It took 170 years for Frederic Williams (Section 3, Block 255) to be reunited with his beloved wife, Mary. Mary died in childbirth in 1845. Williams never recovered from her death and never remarried. Once a successful businessman, he grieved for his wife. (Mary's father, John B. Nelson, had been the proprietor of Nelson's Ferry and was murdered the year she was born by a man who was later declared insane.) Mary was buried in the Nelson family cemetery just north of what is now Fulton County Airport–Brown Field. Frederic spent his years living with his in-laws and later his children; he eventually became an invalid. He was buried in Oakland. When land development took over the Nelson cemetery in 2017, Mary was at last moved to Oakland to rest beside Frederic. (Both, Janice McDonald.)

Gen. Lucius Jeremiah Gartrell (1821–1891). Having already served in both the Georgia and the US House of Representatives, Gen. Lucius Gartrell (Section 3, Block 47) was a well-established lawyer and politician when the Civil War began. He led the 7th Regiment of the Georgia Volunteers. After a year, he went back to politics and was elected to the Confederate Congress, only to return to the lines, where he was wounded. He later made an unsuccessful run for governor. (LOC.)

Dr. Henry Haines Green (1834–1896). Dr. H.H. Green (Section 3, Block 255) advertised his skills of treating "dropsy, in all its various forms." Dropsy is what is now referred to as edema or swelling of tissues. Most of the cures were made of vegetable materials. They were marketed as "Dr. H.H. Green & Son's Chill and Fever Specific." His sons continued the business, starting a successful mail order line. (AHC.)

DROPSY
WITH ALL ITS COMPLICATIONS
TREATED FREE.

DR. H. H. GREEN'S SONS TREAT DROPSY SUCCESSFULLY

TEN DAYS TREATMENT FURNISHED FREE

In order that the patient may realize the great merit of our treatment, after which they can proceed with the treatment or not, as they choose. Some may cry humbug, without knowing anything about it; but remember that it does not cost you anything to realize the great merit of our treatment for yourself.

Send to Dr. H. H. Green's Sons for ten days' treatment, directions and terms. They cure Dropsy in its various forms. Dropsy of the Chest (hydrothorax), generally called heart dropsy; of the Abdomen (acites); Cellular Dropsy (anasarca), known as general dropsy, and other forms of dropsy readily yield to

Maj. John Calhoun Courtney (1834–1899). Maj. John C. Courtney (Section 3, Block 42) began training on the telegraph in Virginia when he was 15. He was the first person to receive telegraphic messages by sound. During the Civil War, Courtney worked directly with Gen. Robert E. Lee in using the telegraph for communication with other leaders of the Confederacy. It was Courtney who delivered word to Jefferson Davis of Pres. Abraham Lincoln's assassination. Courtney came to Atlanta as superintendent of telegraph lines for the Western & Atlantic Railroads. (*Memoirs of Georgia*.)

James Richard Gray (1859–1917). James Gray (Section 6, Block 26) was a practicing lawyer when he took over as editor and publisher of the *Atlanta Journal* newspaper. He bought controlling interest in 1905 and began using the paper to address political and social issues. With his unexpected death, the paper declared him one of American journalism's "greatest editors." The Gray grave is marked with a statue of Niobe, a Greek character who personifies grief. (*Memoirs of Georgia*.)

View in Oakland Cemetery, Atlanta.

Henry Hurt (1814 –1872). Henry Hurt (Section 3, Block 237) was a successful businessman and part of a large entrepreneurial family who moved from Gordon County in the 1860s. Along with brothers Augustus, John, and George Troup, Henry was involved in numerous businesses ventures, including brokering cotton, banking, insurance, real estate, and the railroad. A lifelong bachelor, Henry, along with his family, had numerous properties along the northern edge of the railroad in the Edgewood neighborhood. Henry shared a residence with his thrice-married sister Priscilla Hurt Hudson. When he passed away unexpectedly, he left his estate to his sister. This stereoscopic photograph was taken shortly after his monument was erected in Oakland. Nephew Joel Hurt is known for developing both Inman Park and Druid Hills. (New York Public Library.)

Joel Hurt (1850–1925). One of Atlanta's most successful developers, Joel Hurt (Section 3, Block 237) began his career as a railroad surveyor, surveying the southern route for the Atchison, Topeka & Santa Fe Railway from Albuquerque to Needles, California (now the course of Route 66). He moved to Atlanta in 1875 and helped establish the Atlanta Building and Loan Association and cofounded the Trust Company Bank of Georgia (now part of Truist Financial Corp). In 1885, Hurt founded the East Atlanta Company to create and develop Inman Park with his friend Samuel Inman. He then connected the new neighborhood to downtown Atlanta with an electric trolley system. Hurt also originated the development of Druid Hills. (Both, AHC.)

ER LAWSHE (1824–1897). Er Lawshe (Section 5, Block 109) was a skilled cabinetmaker when he moved to Atlanta. He then trained as a jeweler. He is credited with making the first metal version of the seal of the City of Atlanta. Lawshe's hard work and expanding social circles paid off. Business grew to the point that he was able to build several of what were considered the finest homes on Peachtree. During the Civil War, Lawshe went back north and joined the Union army. While he was gone, the Union army occupied his home, doing considerable damage. He refused to repair some of the shell damage so it could be left as a reminder. Known for his integrity, Lawshe earned the nickname "Old Reliable." (Above, *History of Atlanta*; below, AHC.)

WALTER EMANUEL ORMOND (1875–1909).
Judge Walter Ormond (Section, Block 102) was a popular jurist in Atlanta. While traveling from Savannah to New York, he got seasick and fell overboard. Ormond was a member of the Atlanta Athletic Club and served on the parks commission. His sister Alice Ormond Campbell was a bestselling author and noted women's rights activist. While his body was never found, the Oakland tomb of his mother, Florence Root Ormond (1854–1918), acknowledges him. (*Atlanta Georgian*.)

EDWIN PERCIVAL ANSLEY (1865–1923). Edwin Ansley (Section 3, Block 242) was an attorney but found his passion in real estate. In 1902, he designed and developed Ansley Park, which was called one of the "residential showplaces of the city." It was the first suburb specifically designed to accommodate automobiles. Sensing the importance of having good transportation thoroughfares, he lobbied city council to create Forsythe Street as a crosstown connector through downtown. (*History of Atlanta*.)

GOV. JOSEPH EMERSON BROWN (1821–1894). Gov. Joseph E. Brown (Section 4, Block 99) is considered one of the Georgia's most successful and popular politicians. He was the only governor to serve four terms. South Carolina–born, the Yale-educated attorney prospered in Georgia as a businessman. He was elected governor prior to the outbreak of the Civil War; and as a staunch secessionist, he pushed for Georgia to leave the Union when Abraham Lincoln was elected. Still, he resisted the authority of the central Confederate government, and his disputes with Confederate president Jefferson Davis were legendary. Brown set up a mini welfare system to make sure the necessities of soldiers and civilians alike were met, sending state officials out to make sure the needs were attended to. Postwar, he was pardoned by Pres. Andrew Johnson and helped lead Georgia's Reconstruction efforts. (Left, *Memoirs of Georgia*; below, Judith Vanderver.)

Elizabeth Grisham Brown (1826–1896). Elizabeth Brown (Section 4, Block 99) is depicted in this etching on the side of the monument for her husband, Gov. Joseph E. Brown—a tribute to the celebrated close bond that the couple shared. Mrs. Brown was lauded as being "constantly by his side in all his arduous duties, with aid in toil and wise counsel." The Browns had eight children, including Joseph Mackey Brown (1851–1932) who also served two terms as Georgia governor. The daughter of a Baptist minister, Mrs. Brown was a devout Christian. Her devotion to her husband and what was described as a gentle demeanor made her much beloved by fellow Georgians, as witnessed by the outpouring at her funeral. (Right, Janice McDonald; below, Judith Vandever.)

ELIJAH LEWIS CONNALLY (1837–1930). E.L. Connally (Section 4, Block 99) was one of Atlanta's early physicians. He married Mary Virginia Brown, whose father was Gov. Joseph E. Brown. Connally was part of the first company to join the Confederate Army after South Carolina's secession. He traveled to Pensacola, Florida, to personally enlist with Jefferson Davis. Following the war, he returned to Atlanta and established himself as one of the city's leading doctors and was also heavily involved in real estate development. He is pictured here with his family. From left to right are Mary Temperance Connally (later Mrs. John Schaffner Spalding), Thomas Whipple Connally, Dr. Elijah Lewis Connally, Francis Connally (later Mrs. Hal Fitzgerald Hentz), his wife Mary Virginia Brown Connally, Sally Brown Connally (later Mrs. Hiram Warner Martin), and Joe Brown Connally. (Judith Vanderver.)

SALLY PAT CONNALLY HARDIE (1926–2010).
Sally Pat Hardie (Section 4, Block 99) was a noted environmentalist and philanthropist in both the United States and her adopted Scotland. Born in Atlanta, her great-great-grandfather David Connally was one of the city's earliest settlers, and her great-grandfather Joseph E. Brown was Georgia's governor. After marrying Scotsman Donald Hardie, her influence in the arts, charities, and conservation traversed the Atlantic. She served as a trustee of the National Trust of Scotland, was an ardent supporter of the National Galleries of Scotland, and while on the University Court of St. Andrews University helped develop its internationally renowned sea mammals research unit. A longtime family friend of golfer Bobby Jones, she served as a trustee on his Robert T. Jones Foundation, which arranged exchanges between St. Andrews and Atlanta's Emory University for studies. From left to right are David, Donald, Sally, and Robin Hardie at Buckingham Palace following Donald's being awarded the Order of the British Empire. (Both, Leslye and David Hardie.)

47

MARY BLAIR GLOVER THURMAN (1829–1919). Mary Thurman (Section 3, Block 22) was considered an angel because of her benevolence towards others. She came to Atlanta as the bride of noted dentist Dr. Fendal Dickenson Thurman (1818–1896). Her passion was gardening, and she loved sharing her flowers with friends. She was also known to take bouquets to the sick in local hospitals. (Janice McDonald.)

Grave	Name	Age	Date
1	Harriett H. Green	21	11-30-62
2	William W. Green	-	4-20-55
3	Annie Stokes Wallace	57	4-15-44
4	Edwin Thomas Appleby Jr.	61	1-8-76
5			
6	Henry M. Green	-	7-12-64
7	Henry Fletcher	-	5-19-70
8	Willie Wilson Green	1 yr.	9-30-73
9	Scott Appleby [APPLEBY]	76	10-29-31
10	Hester J. Appleby	68	3/25/1960
11			
12	Fred D. Appleby	52	2-22-23
13	Caroline Green Colt	55	3-5-79
14	Mary Styles Green	71	7-21-74
15	William E. Green	70	4-14-67
16			

HENRY MARTYN GREEN (1829–1864). Sgt. Henry Martyn Green (Section 3 Block 95) died two years before his family purchased the land where he is now buried. Obtaining a 16-grave site, the Greens were among the first to buy into the expanded grounds of the City Cemetery. Sergeant Green was killed during the Civil War near what is now Silver Springs, Maryland. The Works Progress Administration created by Pres. Franklin D. Roosevelt relocated his body to Oakland in the 1930s. (HOF.)

Julius L. Brown (1848–1910). Julius Brown (Section 4, Block 99) enlisted in the Confederate army when he was just 16. Despite his early educational shortcomings, he was later able to finish college with honors, taking law courses at Harvard after the war. Devoted to the law, he turned down a judgeship to continue his practice. Brown helped organize the North Georgia Fair and managed the affairs of the Georgia Mining, Manufacturing and Investment Company. (*Memoirs of Georgia*.)

Theodore Fichter (1840–1897), Katharine Bridgette Rieger Fichter (1850–1911). Theodore and Katharine Fichter (Section 3, Block 43, Lot 3) were both born in Germany, where Theodore trained to be a brewmaster. His skills earned him a reputation and made him sought after by breweries in the United States. He was first hired by a brewery in Cincinnati, Ohio. Then, in 1878, the Steiner Brewery lured him to Atlanta to help start its business. (Janice McDonald.)

MATTHEW ALBERT BEITER (1868–1942). The son of German immigrants, Matthew Beiter (Section 4, Block 116) was born in New York. The family moved to Atlanta, where Matthew fell in love and married Malissa "Minnie" Grubbs. Beiter worked in the publishing industry and was involved in numerous civic organizations, including the Masonic lodge. He was a leader in the Woodmen of the World organization, which turned out to honor him at his funeral. (HOF.)

MALISSA "MINNIE" GRUBBS BEITER (1870–1942). The family of Minnie Beiter (Section 4, Block 116) included some of Atlanta's first residents. Her father, Wilson Lumpkin Grubbs, served in the Confederate army. Minnie was a member of the Merry Needle Club as well as the Order of the Eastern Star. She is shown here with her husband, Matthew, on their wedding day in 1892. She died just two months after the death of her beloved Matthew. (Barb Parks.)

SIDNEY DWIGHT ROOT (1824–1897).
Sidney Root (Section 4, Block 102) became a reluctant secessionist when the Civil War broke out. As a close friend of Confederate president Jefferson Davis, he played several key roles in maintaining the Confederacy, including using his steamships to run blockades and smuggle. Post–Civil War, Root helped rebuild Atlanta both literally and businesswise. He advocated for higher education for African Americans and served as a trustee for both Spelman Seminary and the Atlanta Baptist Seminary (Morehouse College). (*Memoirs of Georgia*.)

JEREMIAH FRANKLIN TROUT (1802–1874).
Jeremiah Trout (Section 5, Block 125) was one of the original Cherokee Land Grant owners in the Atlanta area. He built what was the largest hotel in Atlanta, the four-story Trout Hotel on Decatur Street. The Trout played host to Confederate president Jefferson Davis's visit in 1861 and housed the military during the war. (LOC.)

BENJAMIN FRANKLIN WHITE (1800–1879), THURZA MELVINA GOLIGHTLY WHITE (1805–1878). Maj. Benjamin F. White (Section 4, Block 118) was a journalist, music editor, and musician known as "The Singing Master." He and Elisha James King compiled a book of spiritual music called *The Sacred Harp*. After King's death, White continued to work to have it reissued, and the book is still used by spiritual singers today. He and his wife, Thurza, passed their love of music to their children. Their eighth child, James Landrum White (1847–1925), continued publishing *The Sacred Harp* and faced backlash when he attempted to modernize it. The above photograph of the Whites appears in one edition of *The Sacred Harp*. In the below photograph, J.L. White is shown near his parents' graves. From left to right are J.L., his son James Henry White, nephew Charles E. Clarke, and an unidentified friend. (Left, *Scared Harp*; below, Georgia State Archives.)

Franklin Beatty Davis (1894–1949). Of all of the accolades given Franklin Beatty Davis's (Section 6, Block 62), he was proudest of being a father. In addition to being program director of the Fulton Grand Jury Association, Davis founded the North Fulton Dad's Club. His obituary proclaimed that even after kids outgrew the club, they stayed in touch with Davis, who knew each one by name. He married Mamie Branch Powers (1898–1978) in 1922. (HOF.)

Drury Jenkins Powers (1862–1933). Drury Powers (Section 6, Block 62) followed in his father's footsteps, working at the Southern Railway and Steamship Association. He eventually was appointed its chairman. Drury married Mamie Pauline O'Keefe (1871–1894), and after she and their infant son Drury Paul Powers (1894–1895) died, Drury wed her sister Maude Blanche O'Keefe (1867–1957). Pictured in 1931 are, from left to right, Shirley Powers Davis, Mamie Powers Davis, Virginia Anne Davis, Julia O'Keefe Nelson, Drury Powers, and Maude Powers. (HOF.)

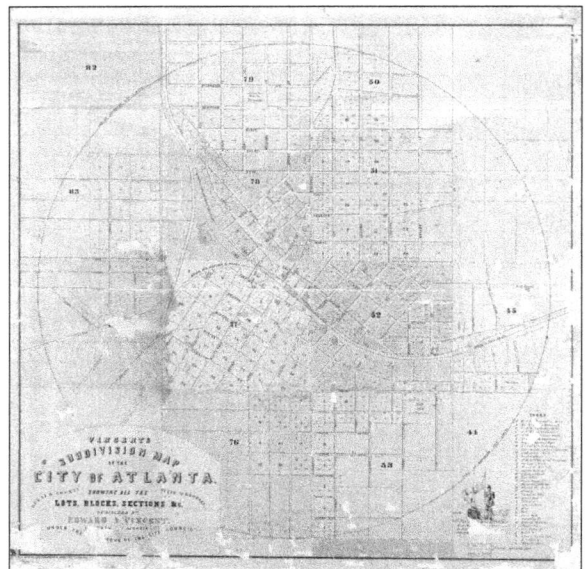

AMMI WILLIAMS (1780–1864). Seeking his fortune in gold, Ammi Williams (Section 6, Bock 85) came to North Georgia in the 1830s following the Dahlonega gold rush and settled in DeKalb County. In 1848, he partnered with Reuben Cone in owning Land Lot 78 of the town that was then called Terminus. That 202.5-acre site lot makes up most of what is now downtown Atlanta. Williams Street is named after Ammi Williams. (LOC.)

LOUISE MARION ODENA (1811–1853). The family of Louise Odena (Section 6, Block 63) says she died of a broken heart. She, her children, and her sister Josephine Marion (1805–1899) moved to Atlanta from South Carolina shortly after the death of Louise's husband, John Hippolyte Odena. The sisters were natives of France. Josephine raised Louise's children after her death, earning money by teaching French. She reportedly hid her nephew Fred in a closet to protect him from Civil War service. (Janice McDonald.)

JOHN THOMAS GRANT (1813–1887).
John Grant (Section 6, Block 57) was a giant in the southern railroad industry as well as being a merchant and a banker. He, his brother James, and the unrelated Lemuel Grant helped build railroads throughout the Southeast. Grant was also a holder of large tracts of land. His grandson John W. Grant was a banker and real estate developer. When John W.'s grandson died at a young age, he funded the development of what is now known as Bobby Dodd Stadium at Georgia Tech's historic Grant Field. They are all in the Grant mausoleum, as are Gov. John Slaton (1866–1955) and his wife, Sarah Frances (1870–1945). Governor Slaton is remembered for the Leo Frank trial, in which he changed Franks's sentence from death to life in prison; after Frank was lynched, Slaton was never elected to public office again. (Right, *Memoirs of Georgia*; below, AHC.)

Dr. Daniel Cornelius O'Keefe (1828–1871). Irish-born Dr. Daniel O'Keefe (Section 6, Block 62) studied medicine in Augusta. Moving to Atlanta, he filled two chairs in the Atlanta Medical College and served on the city board of health. During the Civil War, he was a surgeon for the Confederacy. As city alderman in 1869, he introduced a resolution that led to the establishment of public schools for the city of Atlanta. (HOF.)

Dr. Joseph Payne Logan (1821–1891). Dr. Joseph Logan (Section 7, Lot 372) was one of Atlanta's first trained medical doctors. Numerous accounts of the Civil War's 1864 Battle of Atlanta take note of his heroic and compassionate efforts to treat the wounded and ease their suffering. As a teacher at the Medical College, Dr. Logan also helped to organize the Atlanta Memorial Association in 1866 to honor and bury the Confederate dead. Dr. Logan was the association's first president. (Janice McDonald.)

REBECCA DOUGLAS LOWE (1844–1918). Rebecca Douglas Lowe (Section 6, Block 82) was a trailblazer in the effort to improve the plight of working women, pushing for education and equal pay. She helped form and became the first president of the Atlanta Women's Club. In 1896, she invited 17 other women's clubs to come together and created the Georgia Federation of Women's Clubs. A year later, Lowe became its president as well. She was elected president of the General Federation of Women in 1898 at the national convention in Colorado. Lowe is credited with urging women to work together for their own advancement, including her personal vow to "take up the trouble of the working woman and see what we can do to lighten her labor and increase her pay." (General Federation of Women.)

WILLIAM ALLEN RAWSON (1810–1879). W.A. Rawson (Section 7, Block 30) built his considerable fortune manufacturing books, paper, and stationery. He also amassed a great amount of real estate. Rawson helped design his exotic Gothic revival architectural-style mausoleum, which he wanted to be a standout at Oakland. It was completed a year after his death. Among those resting with him are his wife, Julia (1818–1865), daughter Susan Julia Eliza Collier (1854–1897), and her husband, Atlanta mayor Charles Augustus Collier (1848–1900). Collier was president of the Cotton States and International Exposition Company and planned Atlanta's 1895 Cotton States International Exposition. He died tragically after being shot while searching for a burglar in his backyard. (Left, *Memoirs of Georgia*, below, Janice McDonald.)

Julian LaRose Harris (1874–1963), Julia Florida Collier Harris (1875–1967). Julian and Julia Harris (Section 7, V6, Block 3) were true partners, both personally and professionally. Julia was the daughter of Atlanta mayor Charles Collier, while Julian was the son of beloved folklorist Joel Chandler Harris. Julian started his career at age 16 reporting for the *Atlanta Journal-Constitution*. He was managing editor by the time he met Julia, when she returned to Atlanta after attending art school in Boston. Together, they worked to call attention to social injustices. After Julian's service in World War I, they purchased the *Columbus Enquirer-Sun*. In 1926, their reporting on the activities of the Ku Klux Klan helped earn them a Pulitzer Prize. Julia wrote the first biography of her father-in-law, called *The Life and Letters of Joel Chandler Harris*. (Both, AHC.)

DR. ABNER WELLBORN CALHOUN (1845–1910). Dr. Abner Calhoun (Section 7, Block 343) was founder of the Emory Eye Clinic. Calhoun was intrigued by the causes of blindness and other sight issues, and he traveled to Europe to study diseases of the eye. When he returned to Atlanta, Dr. Calhoun was the only scientifically trained ophthalmologist in the South. He taught at the Atlanta Medical College (now Emory University School of Medicine), which had been established by his father, Andrew B. Calhoun. (*History of Georgia*.)

GORDON BURTON SMITH (1889–1909). Gordon Smith (Section 7 Block 341) was the grandson of two former Georgia governors, Hoke Smith and John B. Gordon. Known for his athleticism and his engineering skills, Smith played fullback for the legendary football coach John Heisman at Georgia Tech. The engineering student went to Panama in the summer of 1909 to work with the railroad during the building of the canal. He drowned when the canoe he was traveling in on the Chagres River was swamped. (Janice McDonald.)

THOMAS PENDLETON WESTMORELAND (1840–1914). T.P. Westmoreland (Section 7, Block 7) and three of his brothers served in the Civil War; T.P. served with Hampton's Legion. His obituary proclaimed that postwar, "he came to this city to cast his lot with a hearty handful who had faith in Atlanta's future." Westmoreland made his name as a judge in criminal trials. Known for his piety, he was a steward of Trinity Church for over 30 years. (*Memoirs of Georgia.*)

FRANK PLUMMER RICE (1838–1923). Involved in everything from stonecutting to railroads, Frank Rice (Section 7, Block 9) successfully lobbied to move the state capital from Milledgeville to Atlanta. He worked to help establish the Atlanta Public School System. Rice served in the general assembly as well as being elected to the Georgia State Senate. (*Memoirs of Georgia.*)

SAMUEL MARTIN INMAN (1843–1915). In 1889, Samuel Inman (Section 7, Block 8) owned the largest cotton mill in Atlanta, S.W. Inman & Co.; it also had a branch in Houston, Texas. He was one of the wealthiest people in Atlanta. Inman partnered with Joel Hurt to establish the new neighborhood east of downtown that would come to be known as Inman Park. They also developed as the Atlanta and Edgewood Street Railway. Convincing Richard Peters to donate land for the school, Inman was among the first to donate money towards establishing the Georgia School of Technology. He was often referred to as "Atlanta's First Citizen." (AHC.)

EUGENIA JONES BACON (1840–1920). Eugenia Bacon (Section 7, Block 4) and her husband, Oliver (1835–1873), fled their Liberty County plantation following the Civil War. Her husband and their son died of typhoid, leaving her destitute. Working as a traveling companion and art teacher, she traveled extensively throughout Europe and Russia. Bacon gained notoriety with her novel *Lyddy: A Tale of the Old South*, a fictionalized version of her life on a plantation. (Georgia Archives.)

ALFRED AUSTELL (1814–1881). One of the largest cotton dealers of his time, Alfred Austell (Section 7, Lot 373) was also known for building banks and railroads. Austell was a cashier at the National Bank of Fulton in 1858 when he helped establish both the Atlanta National Bank and the Atlanta Savings Bank. A supporter of transportation initiatives, he built the Atlanta and Charlotte Air-Line as well as the Spartanburg–Asheville branch of what later became the Southern Railway. (Janice McDonald.)

MOSES FORMWALT (1820–1852). Moses Formwalt (Section 10) was Atlanta's first mayor. He was a tinsmith making stills in 1848 when he ran for the position under the Free and Rowdy political party. During his one-year term, he earned praise for cutting more roads and building Atlanta's first jail. Formwalt was stabbed to death by a prisoner while serving as deputy sheriff. Originally buried elsewhere, he was reinterred at this monument. (Janice McDonald.)

THOMAS MOORE CLARK (1828–1917). Thomas Clark (Section 7, Block 3) was a leading hardware merchant in Atlanta when he purchased a lot at Oakland in 1869. This deed shows he paid $100 for two lots in Block 3 on land that had been purchased in 1866 for the cemetery expansion. The deed is signed not just by Clark but also by Atlanta mayor William Hulsey. (AHC.)

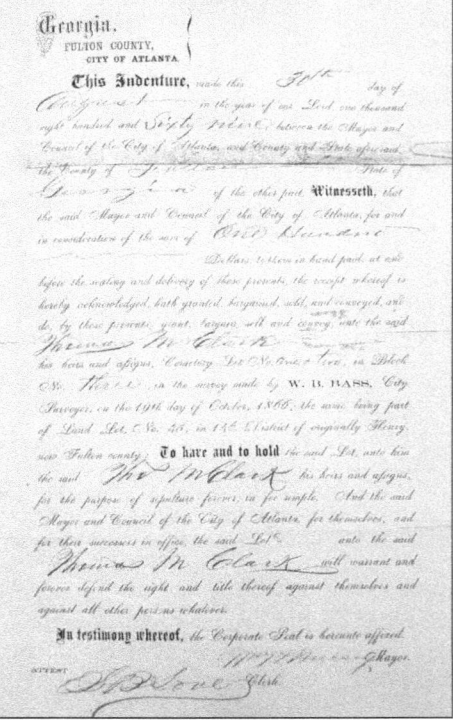

Henry Patillo Farrow (1834–1907). Unlike the rest of his family, Henry Farrow (Section 7, Block 8) opposed secession and helped form a Union Association in 1860 to stand against it. When he was finally forced to join the Confederate army, he was in charge of procuring the materials for manufacturing munitions. His sympathetic leanings towards Republicans during Reconstruction earned him an appointment as state attorney general under Gov. Rufus Bullock. (HOF.)

Col. Robert Flournoy Maddox (1829–1899). Following the war, Col. Robert F. Maddox (Section 6, Block 56) used his position in the legislature to seek food resources for the state. He used connections to start produce and cotton brokerages as well as the Maddox-Rucker Baking Company. A reported 70 of the most prominent leaders of the community were among his funeral escorts to Oakland. (AHC.)

SAMUEL HOYT VENABLE (1856–1939). Samuel Venable (Section 7, Block 243), along with his brother William, purchased Stone Mountain in 1887 from several different owners. They were the first to own the entire mountain. While most know it just as Stone Mountain Park, this massive granite outcropping included the Venable Brothers quarry, from which stone was cut and shipped throughout the United States. The steps of the US Capitol and the foundation of the Lincoln Memorial come from Stone Mountain. Venable worked with the Daughters of the Confederacy to commission a massive carving of Confederate generals on the side of the mountain. This is a rendering of the larger original plan. The unmarried Venable died before it was completed and left his half of the mountain to his niece Elizabeth Venable Mason. (Both, AHC.)

Judge Cicero Henry Strong (1828–1897). Judge C.H. Strong (Section 6, Block 78) was described as "massive in frame and tall in stature." He was admired by constituents and colleagues alike. Strong's family traced its roots to England and then New England. The family had a history in politics and the law, so Strong saw becoming a lawyer as a legacy. Judge Strong was involved in the first court created in the new county of Fulton in 1853. (*History of Georgia.*)

MR. CHARLES BEERMANN.

Charles Beerman (1833–1896). Charles Beerman (Section 11, Block 218) immigrated to the United States from Germany. While his love was raising and selling songbirds, the enterprising Beerman made a name for himself first in selling cigars and tobacco. He later was an officer in the Atlanta Brewing and Ice Company, serving first as its treasurer and then as its president. Beerman died while traveling in Austria but had requested to be buried in Atlanta. AHC.)

Dr. Pierre Paul Noel D'Alvigny (1800–1877). Dr. Pierre D'Alvigny (Section 10 Block 130) was born in Paris and came to the United States after serving as a surgeon's assistant in the Napoleonic Wars. He first practiced dentistry in New York before moving to Charleston and then Atlanta. While too old to volunteer for the Civil War, D'Alvigny offered his services as a surgeon during the Siege of Atlanta. He is credited with saving the Atlanta Medical College from being burned by General Sherman's men in 1864 by convincing them it was full of wounded patients. D'Alvigny was known to work with the African American community, even taking a post in a hospital that only treated blacks. (Georgia State Archives.)

THOMAS F. STOCKS (1871–1943). Thomas Stock (Section 10, Block 139) is pictured at the funeral of his wife, Diamond Edward Stocks (1873–1913), at Oakland. He was part owner of the Stocks Coal Company, serving as its general manager, treasurer, and secretary. Stocks was elected in 1903 as the first water commissioner for the City of Atlanta, serving two terms. There is a plaque honoring him at the City of Atlanta Water Tower. (Kelly Stocks.)

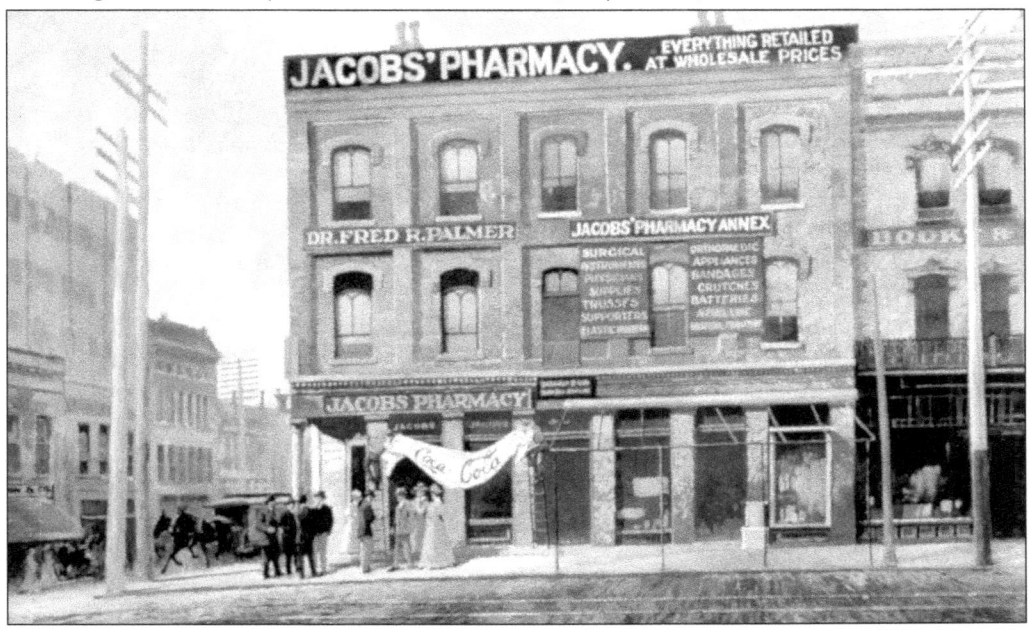

WILLIS ERWIN VENABLE (1842 –1920). Owning Atlanta's first soda fountain, W.E. Venable (Section 11, Block 150) had the nickname "Soda Water King of the South." He is created with carbonating a caramel-colored headache and handover syrup that his friend Dr. John Pemberton concocted, thus serving up the first ever version of Coca-Cola. Venable sold out his share of the business before it became a success. (Coca-Cola.)

JACOB EISEMAN (1842–1920). Jacob Eiseman (Section 12, Block 748) fought in the Battle of Atlanta, losing three fingers in the conflict. He became a builder, constructing many buildings in Atlanta, including the Central State Hospital. Eiseman first purchased the family lot at Oakland after his son Charlie (1871–1893) was killed in a hunting accident. Eiseman is pictured at center with his grandchildren, from left to right, Alfred Lynne Brannen, Mildred Brannen, and T.H. Brannen Jr. (HOF.)

PROCORUS SCOTT THORNTON (1859–1897). P. Scott Thornton (Section 11, Block 189) spent his life in pursuit of the stage. His death was a painful one from an undiagnosed illness, but his career reviews were equally excruciating. In a scathing obituary, friends lamented how Thornton's talents were mocked by others. They recounted how "a cabbage whizzed by his head at the most solemn moment of his soliloquy" and "eggs splashed over the footlights" as people jeered his performance. (HOF.)

THOMAS HENRY BRANNEN (1869–1941). T.H. Brannen (Section 12, Block 748) said he was "answering the call of the city" when he moved to Atlanta from tiny Zebulon, Georgia. He began working with a local druggist and eventually became a buyer for Jacob's drugstore. He then started his own company. At one time, T.H. Brannen and Anthony Pharmacy was one of the largest in Atlanta. Brannen served as president of the Georgia Pharmaceutical Association. (HOF.)

ABBIE HOWARD (1830–1905). Abbie Howard (Section 12, Block 265) was madam of one of Atlanta's best-known bordellos following the Civil War. She had entered the "world's oldest profession" after moving from Louisiana. Howard quickly created her own establishment, becoming known in the community both for run-ins with the law and her charity. The character Belle Watling in Gone with the Wind is said to be modeled after Howard. (Janice McDonald.)

JAMES LAFAYETTE DICKEY SR. (1847–1910). The wealthy Buckhead neighborhood's massive estates had their beginnings thanks to James L. Dickey Sr. (Section 15, Lot 219). The Dickey family owned a farm in Fannin County where a group of developers discovered what they described as the best marble in America. They offered a 100-year lease on the land to quarry the marble, guaranteeing the family a handsome income. Dickey moved to Atlanta, where he became a businessman and civic leader. He spent $6,000 and bought 403 acres of lush woodlands north of downtown to use as a retreat. This area is now Buckhead. Dickey sold large tracts of his property to his successful businessmen friends who built expansive estates there. Among them were Robert F. Maddox, William Henry Kiser, and William Baily Lamar. (Both, Janice McDonald.)

Three
AFRICAN AMERICAN GROUNDS

WILLIAM FINCH (1832–1911). William Finch (Section 15, Block 73) was born a slave in Augusta and moved to Atlanta as a freedman. It is believed his father was Georgia chief justice J.H. Lumpkin, to whom he was close. At the height of Reconstruction, Finch was elected as Atlanta's first black city councilman. A staunch supporter of education, he helped found Atlanta's first school system. (Kamaria Finch.)

JEFFERSON ALEXANDER CAREY SR. (1825–1890). After obtaining his freedom, Jefferson Carey Sr. (Block 15, Lot 76, Grave 3) became a sharecropper in Upton County. Instead of making money from his work, somehow, he owed money to the landowner. Carey moved his family to Atlanta for a better life. Working in a restaurant and as a driver, he made enough money to purchase a home. He was also ordained as a church elder. (Janice McDonald.)

CHRISTOPHER COLUMBUS WIMBISH JR. (1892–1963). Atlanta-born C.C. Wimbish Jr. (Section 18, Block 32) spent his adult life in Chicago, having graduated law school from Northwestern University. He served as Illinois's assistant state's attorney as well as assistant corporation counsel for the City of Chicago. In 1942, Wimbish was elected to the Illinois State Senate, where he sponsored the Fair Employment Practices bill. The bill did not become law until 1962. Here, Illinois state senator John J. Parish is second from right, and Wimbish is seated center with unidentified fellow lawmakers. (Abraham Lincoln Library.)

Dr. Roderick Duke Badger (1834–1890). Dr. R.D. Badger (Section 18, Block 52) was the first African American dentist in Atlanta. Born to prominent white slave owner Dr. Joshua Badger and slave Martha Badger, he was taught dentistry by his father at age 16 and opened his practice in Atlanta in 1854. During the Civil War, he served as an aid to Confederate captain Milton Candler (brother of Coca-Cola founder Asa Candler). Badger returned to dentistry after the war. His successful downtown practice was a block away from that of his white half brother, Ralph Badger. Well respected and active in the community, R.D. Badger was named the first black trustee of Clark University, helped establish the Freedman's Savings and Trust, and in 1872 was chosen as a District Six alternative delegate to the Democratic National Convention. (Above, Janice McDonald; right, The Negro History Bulletin.)

CARRIE STEELE LOGAN (1829–1900). Carrie Logan (Block 64, Lot 5, Grave No. 2) was born a slave, but unlike most at that time, she learned to read and write. While working as the maid at Atlanta's Union Station, she began caring for the homeless black children who were hanging around the trains. She solicited funding and in 1888 built the first orphanage for black children in Georgia. The Carrie Steele-Pitts Home remains the oldest predominately black orphanage in the United States. (Carrie Steel-Pitts Orphan Home.)

OLLIVETTE EUGENIA SMITH ALLISON (1924–2010). Although she never gave birth, Ollivette Allison (1924–2010) (Block 64, Lot 5) mothered thousands of children. In 1936, she was 12 years old when she and two brothers were sent to Atlanta's Carrie Steele-Pitts Home after their parents divorced. Home founder Carrie Pitts allowed Allison to stay after she became an adult. She served first as a social worker then worked 32 years as home director. A collector of elephant figurines, her headstone pays tribute to her love of the gentle creatures. (Janice McDonald.)

Bishop Wesley John Gaines (1840–1912). A former slave, Bishop Wesley Gaines (Section 18, Block 65) became the second pastor of the Old Bethel African Methodist Episcopal Church. Passionate about education, he helped found the Morris Brown College of the AME Church, the only college in Georgia exclusively for African Americans. He was also vice president of Payne Theological Seminary. (LOC.)

Eli Olin Wimby (1889–1918). Eli Olin Wimby (Section 18, Block 56) was a doorman at Atlanta's Daniel Department Store when World War I erupted. He was serving as a private in the Labor Battalion in France when he developed pneumonia and died. His body was brought back to Atlanta three years after his death for his burial in Oakland. He was posthumously awarded the French Certificate of Honor. (Janice McDonald.)

REV. JOSEPH A. WOODS (1823–1903). Rev. Joseph Woods (Section 18, Block 5) was the first pastor of the Big Bethel AME Church, which had its beginning as Union Church in 1847 in the newly formed Marthasville. After the end of the Civil War, Union Church evolved into being called Bethel African Methodist Episcopal Church. Woods was instrumental in helping open Gate City Colored School, the first public school for blacks in Atlanta. It operated in the church basement. (Janice McDonald.)

SOLOMON LUCKIE (?–1864). One of the final casualties of the Siege of Atlanta, Solomon Luckie was standing in front of his barbershop when he was struck by shrapnel from a Union shell. He died from his injuries soon afterwards. Luckie and his wife, Nancy, were among fewer than 45 freed blacks living in Atlanta. He had operated a successful barbershop and bathhouse at the Atlanta Hotel at the corner of Alabama and Whitehall Streets. Luckie is buried in an unmarked grave. (AHC.)

CHARLES A. FAISON (1871–1936). The obituary for Charles Faison (Section 15, Block 52) describes him as a "self-made man," "active citizens" and "ideal husband and devoted Christian." Faison was a longtime partner of Georgia's first black millionaire, Alonzo Herndon, managing the Herndon Barbershop. The celebrated flagship shop at 66 Peachtree Street was often called "The Crystal Palace" and served prominent white customers. Faison was also on the board of the Atlanta Life Insurance Company. (Alonzo Herndon Home.)

MYRA MILLER (1811–1891). Myra Miller (Section 18, Block 22) was a highly sought-after caterer and baker in the late 1800s, known for what were referred to as her "edible works of art." She married a white doctor in Rome before the couple moved to Atlanta, where Myra established herself as a premier baker. The Atlanta papers' social pages regularly highlighted the works of wonder she created for events, especially weddings. (Janice McDonald.)

Dr. Henry Rutherford Butler (1862–1931). Dr. Henry Rutherford Butler (Section 18, Block 68) and Selena Sloan Butler were an Atlanta power couple, known as gracious and gifted leaders whose influences are still felt today. They met and married soon after Selena graduated Spelman College. Married 40 years, they shared a passion for each other, their community, interracial cooperation, and European travel. A graduate of Meharry Medical School, Dr. Butler established one of the city's first African American medical practices as well as the first black-owned pharmacy in Georgia. He was a founder of the Association of Physicians, Pharmacists, and Dentists of Georgia and was one of the founders of both the Atlanta Medical Association and the National Medical Association. Considered a mentor to many young men, he was instrumental in founding the Butler Street YMCA. He was also director of the Atlanta State Savings Bank. (Auburn Avenue Research Library.)

SELENA SLOAN BUTLER (1872–1964).
Selena Sloan Butler (Section 18, Block 68) was a passionate educator and child welfare advocate. Concerned over the ability of her only child, Henry Rutherford Jr., to get a good education, she enlisted other mothers involved in their children's studies. Unable to find a kindergarten for her son, she started one in her own home. The next year, she followed her students into their grammar school at Yonge Street. Butler founded the Georgia Colored Parent-Teacher Association. It expanded to the National Congress of Colored Parents and Teachers Association in 1911, the first parent-teacher organization for African Americans in the United States. She later helped create the National Congress of Parents and Teachers, now a part of the National Parent Teacher Association (PTA). After her husband died, she traveled to Europe where she worked with the British Nursery School Association before returning to the United States. (Both, Auburn Avenue Research Library.)

OLIVE A. TAYLOR (1881–1932). Olive Taylor (Section 18, Block 72) was principal at the Yonge Street School in the early 1900s, where she dealt with the issue that many of her students were only attending class half the time. In 1911, Taylor joined forces with Selena Sloan Butler to create a parent-teacher association for African Americans to address the attendance problem. The idea of a PTA spread to other schools, and theirs was the precursor to the National PTA. (Janice McDonald.)

MARIE WOOLFOLK TAYLOR (1893–1960). Just one generation from slavery, Marie Woolfolk Taylor (Section 18, Block 52) helped establish the first Greek letter sorority for black women. The Atlanta native was attending Howard University in Washington in 1908 when she and eight others created the Alpha Kappa Alpha Sorority. She was AKA's first secretary. Graduating magna cum laude, Taylor returned to Atlanta and was active in her church and her community. She was involved in numerous civic organizations, including the NAACP. (Janice McDonald.)

Dr. Fred B. Palmer (1834–1919). Dr. Fred Palmer (Section 18, Block 45) was a white physician and son of a slave owner when, while working at Jacob's Pharmacy, he fell in love with former slave Julia Hays (1851–1916). The two defied convention and married. Records of the time indicate that he demanded his wife be treated with the respect of any other doctor's spouse. Palmer created a skin-whitening cream, advertising it in black newspapers throughout the country. After Julia's death, laws dictated she be buried in the African America section. Palmer chose to be buried beside her. A version of Palmer's whitening cream still sells today, as does Palmer's Cocoa Butter, which bears his name. (*Kansas City Sun* 1919.)

Dr. Loring Brainard Palmer (1875–1935). Dr. L.B. Palmer (Section 18, Block 47) followed in his father's footsteps in the medical field, graduating from Atlanta University and then the University of Pennsylvania's medical school. He became a noted surgeon as well as a civil rights activist, working alongside W.E.B. Du Bois. Palmer participated in several conferences involving race relations, including the Annual Conference for the Study of the Negro Problems. (New York Public Library.)

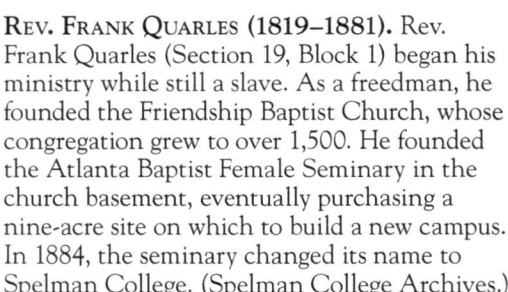

Rev. Frank Quarles (1819–1881). Rev. Frank Quarles (Section 19, Block 1) began his ministry while still a slave. As a freedman, he founded the Friendship Baptist Church, whose congregation grew to over 1,500. He founded the Atlanta Baptist Female Seminary in the church basement, eventually purchasing a nine-acre site on which to build a new campus. In 1884, the seminary changed its name to Spelman College. (Spelman College Archives.)

AUGUSTUS THOMPSON (1837–1910). Augustus Thompson (Section 18, Block 60) was born to a freed father and slave mother in Mississippi. He came to Georgia when his mother was willed to a man in Madison while his father was forced to stay behind. Thompson trained as a blacksmith, later becoming a master smithy. When the Civil War erupted, he worked at the Confederate Gun Factory Company in Lexington and the Augusta Machine Works in Augusta making guns for Confederate troops. After the war, he used his newfound freedom to open his own blacksmith shop in Atlanta. Following his failed bid for city council, Thompson emerged as a community leader. He organized the St. James Lodge of the Odd Fellows, the first African American lodge of the fraternal organization. (HOF.)

Thomas E. Askew (1847–1914). As Atlanta's first African American photographer, Thomas Askew (Section 18, Block 36) is credited with taking some of the most iconic photographs of noted black Atlantans at the turn of the 20th century. A master of lighting and composition, Askew created work that was heavily featured in W.E.B. Du Bois's Exhibit of American Negroes at the 1900 World's Fair in Paris. This photograph is a self-portrait. Three years after Askew's death, the Great Atlanta Fire destroyed his equipment and most of his work. (LOC.)

Antoine Graves Sr. (1862–1941). A prominent real estate broker, Antoine Graves Sr. (Section 18, Block 65) ran a business housed in the celebrated Kimball Building amid mostly white businessmen. The Georgia capitol stands on land for which Graves brokered the deal. He was also the principal of the Storrs School, the first school for blacks run entirely by a black administration. Graves's is the only mausoleum in the African American section and holds eight family members. (Janice McDonald.)

MALCOLM CLAIBORNE (1838–1870). This statue on the Georgia capitol grounds pays tribute to Malcolm Claiborne and a group of more than two dozen African American legislators elected in 1868. Members of the group were denied their seats by white legislators. It took almost two years and federal intervention, but in 1870, the men were able to take their elected positions. Claiborne's time in office was cut short. Not long after assuming his seat, he got in a heated argument with the House messenger over House pages and was shot to death. Claiborne's final resting place at Oakland is not known. (Janice McDonald.)

Dr. Blanche Beatrice Bowman Thompson (1880–1964). Dr. Blanche Thompson (Section 15, Block 1, Lot 2) was the first black surgeon in Athens, Georgia, where she treated both black and white patients. She also established her own sanitarium for the treatment of tuberculosis. A graduate of Meharry Medical College, she had taught at Knoxville Medical College, where her husband, Sydney James Thompson (d. 1945), was one of her students. He never completed his medical training, instead becoming a baker. The couple relocated to Atlanta, where Sydney became a probation officer. He also founded the first Black Boys Club in Atlanta. Sharing their lot are Dr. Thompson's sister Estella Amelia Bowman Henderson (1887–1936) and her husband, Fred R. Henderson (d. 1958). In 1919, Estella passed the Alabama bar and practiced law in Georgia. She served on the faculty of Morris Brown. Fred was a carpenter who studied in Tuskegee under Booker T. Washington. (Janice McDonald.)

HENRY ALLEN RUCKER (1852–1924). Henry Rucker (Section 18, Block 48) rose from slavery to become one of the first African American to be appointed to the Internal Revenue Service in the state of Georgia. He is shown here at his office at the IRS. Educated at the Storrs School, Rucker used his position as a barber to advise and earn the trust of white businessmen. He grew to become a leader in the Georgia State Loan and Trust Company. Rucker was a delegate several times to the Republican National Convention, befriending Sen. William McKinley and helping push for his election as president. In 1890, Rucker helped to form the Georgia Real Estate and Trust Company. (LOC.)

MAYNARD JONES WARTMAN (1892–1954). Maynard Wartman (Section 18, Block 68) was part of the only African American Signal Corps group of World War II. Company C of the 325th Field Signal Battalion is shown here stringing wire in the no-man's-land of France's Argonne Forest in 1918. A student at Brown University when he enlisted, Wartman returned to complete his degree. He taught chemistry at Morehouse College before becoming an agent for Atlanta Life Insurance Company. (National Archives.)

JESSIE MURPHY WARTMAN (1894–1980). Jessie Wartman (Section 18, Block 48) was an Atlanta Public Schools music educator. She helped organize the first elementary school bands of the City Schools of Atlanta as well as a yearly citywide choral performance by elementary school students. She was a 1916 graduate of Atlanta University. (Janice McDonald.)

Four
JEWISH GROUNDS

DAVID MAYER (1815–1890). In 1860, David Mayer helped secure land in the Atlanta Cemetery on behalf of the Hebrew Benevolent Association (now the Hebrew Benevolent Congregation) so that the growing Jewish community could have consecrated land on which to be buried. Mayer trained as a dentist in his native Germany before immigrating to the United States in 1847. One of the first Jewish settlers in Atlanta, he helped found the Atlanta Board of Education. Despite the Oakland connection, Mayer is buried in Westview Cemetery. (HOF.)

AARON HAAS (1841–1912). Aaron Haas (Section, 16, Bock 276) was part of the first Jewish family to live in Atlanta. He was founding member of what became Hebrew Benevolent Congregation (The Temple) and worked with David Mayer to lobby the Atlanta City Council to give land in Oakland Cemetery for Jewish burials. He helped broker Confederate cotton during the Civil War to pay for the cause and was captured while running a blockade to England; he bribed his jailer to escape. Haas served on the Atlanta City Council, then as mayor pro tem before becoming a trustee in the city waterworks. He was a founding member of the Piedmont Driving Club, which later actually banned Jews. He was grand president of the Fifth District Grand Lodge of B'nai B'rith and helped found the Hebrew Orphan's Home. He married Fannie Rich (1857–1949), whose family founded Rich's Department Store. (Breman Museum.)

DR. HENRY BAK (1846–1915). Dr. Henry Bak (Section 16, Block 1) was one of the first Jewish doctors to practice in Atlanta. Born in Hungary, he came to Atlanta via New York. In addition to being a well-respected physician, Dr. Bak was fluent in several languages and was lauded for his linguistic skills. When he retired, he moved to Chicago but requested that his burial take place in Oakland Cemetery. (Janice McDonald.)

MARTIN MENKO (1821–1883). Martin Menko (Section 17, Block 279) was 38 years old when he married 18-year-old Caroline Oberdorf (1824–1880). They came to America from Bavaria along with Martin's brother Joseph. The Menko brothers started working as peddlers when they arrived, eventually making enough to buy a store. So respected was Martin that when he died, other clothing stores closed so that everyone could attend his services. Menko was a charter member of the new temple in Atlanta. (Janice McDonald.)

ABRAHAM ROSENFELD (1828–1904), EMILIE BAER ROSENFELD (1845–1923). Abraham Rosenfeld (Section 17, Block 278) married Emilie Bare in 1867 in the first Jewish wedding performed in Atlanta. The Reverend Isaac Leeser of Philadelphia presided over the nuptials. Leeser used the occasion to encourage those gathered to create a more permanent Jewish congregation. Within four months, the Hebrew Benevolent Congregation had formed and work had begun to build a synagogue. (Breman Museum.)

Julius Regenstein (1826–1920), Matilda Kutz Regenstein (1845–1929). Julius and Matilda Regenstein (Section 17, Block 270) came to Atlanta in 1871 and established the first millinery school in the South, creating hats that were coveted by women throughout the United States. Julius partnered with his brother Gabriel (1823–1897), and they started Regenstein Bros. Surprise Store on Whitehall Street. Regenstein's Department Store was known for its fine ladies' fashion and was the first to hire women to help customers. It was a family operation, and various sons, daughters, and cousins held different positions in the company right up until it was sold in the 1970s. This advertisement in *Illustrated Milliner* from 1920 pays tribute to Julius after his death by showing him (center) surrounded by sons Louis (1878–1965), Seligman (1871–1931), Meyer (1869–1933), and Joseph (1874–1946). (*Illustrated Milliner.*)

RHODA KAUFMAN (1888–1956). Rhoda Kaufman (Section J-2, Lot 45) was a social worker and activist, serving on almost every city and state welfare organization. In 1923, she was appointed executive secretary of Georgia's Department of Public Welfare. Pres. Herbert Hoover invited her to participate in the White House Conference on Child Health and Protection. Upon retiring, Kaufman joined the United Nation's Women's Organization and the League of Women Voters. (HOF.)

YOEL LYONS JOEL (1896–1918). Yoel Joel (Section 16, Lot 78) grew up as the son of a dry goods store owner in downtown Atlanta. He attended the University of Georgia and was called into service in World War I, training at Fort McPherson. While leading his men against German positions in Argonne, France, Lieutenant Joel was mortally wounded, dying sometime later. Originally interred in the American Cemetery in Nantes, his family arranged to have him brought to the family vault in Oakland. He was posthumously cited for his bravery in battle. (HOF.)

MORRIS RICH (1847–1929), EMANUEL RICH (1849–1897), DANIEL RICH (1844–1920). Morris Rich (Section 17, Block 277) first opened a dry goods store at 36 Whitehall Street (now Peachtree Street) in Atlanta in 1867. By the time his brother Emanuel (pictured right, Section 17, Block 277, Lot 93) joined him, M. Rich's & Company was the fifth-largest store in Atlanta and had moved to a much larger building. When brother Daniel entered the firm (1844–1920), M. Rich & Brothers more than doubled in size. The Riches prided themselves in catering to middle-class customers. Emanuel Rich (pictured here) personally was involved in picking out many of the imported items, often bringing them back with him to avoid shipping costs. In 1929, the company simply became known as Rich's and grew to become one of the largest retail chains in the Southeast. The company remained family operated until it was sold to Federated Department Stores in 1976. (Both, AHC.)

Louis Cohen (1849–1937). Louis Cohen (Section 16, Block J-2) was born in Germany and moved with his family to Americus, Georgia, at the age of three. An entrepreneur, he shaped the town of Sandersville and its surroundings. Cohen started in business with a general merchandise store before moving on to sell cotton and later establishing the Banking House of Louis Cohen. He was president of the Sandersville & Tennille Railway and established the Sandersville & Tennille Telephone exchange, which eventually merged with Southern Bell Telephone Company. At one time, he even owned the Birmingham Guano Company. Cohen installed the first electric light system in the community and worked to develop a waterworks and sewage system for the city. He also served as an alderman and mayor of Sandersville as well as serving 30 years on the board of education. Lauded for his generosity and mourned for his loss, Cohen was buried in Oakland because there were no Jewish burial grounds in his beloved Sandersville. (Davie Lemer Davis.)

ANNIE HAPP COHEN (1853–1921). Annie Cohen (Section 16, Block J-2) grew up in Sandersville as the daughter of prominent merchant Pinkus Happ, who owned the local general store. Her father endeared himself to the community during the Civil War by using his means to help others in their time of need. Annie Happ married Louis Cohen and was known in the community for her support of him in his civic endeavors. (Davie Lemer Davis.)

FLORENCE COHEN LIBERMAN (1880–1966). As a child in Sandersville, Florence Cohen Liberman (Section 16, Block 46) loved to perform. Her father, Louis Cohen, built a bandstand on the courthouse grounds where she sang with the "Florence Symphony." Florence graduated in 1897 from Wesleyan College and married Isaac Lieberman (1876–1948), who worked in furniture sales and divided time between Sandersville and Atlanta. From left to right are Florence Cohen Lieberman, Louis Lieberman (1905–1914), Annie Happ Cohen (Lemer), and Davie Bach Cohen. (Davie Lemer Davis.)

WILLIAM TITLEBAUM (1819–1896). William Titlebaum (Section 9, Block 469) emigrated from Austria and opened a dry goods store in the new town of Atlanta. His advertisements bragged about his ability to make a wide selection of hoop skirts. He also sold corsets, millinery goods, hosiery, and white and fancy goods. Titlebaum is pictured here in the center with his daughter Julia (1851–1948) directly in front of him. Julia later married Daniel Rich of Rich's Department Store. In the back row are, from left to right, Theodore Eichberg, William Titlebaum, David Bach, Josephine Lieberman (later Mrs. David Kaufman), Julia Titlebaum (later Mrs. Dan Rich), and Dora Dewald (later Mrs. Henry Cohen). (Davie Lemer Davis.)

HERMAN A. LEMER (1903–1957). Herman Lemer (Section 16, Block 84) was born in Boston and raised in Newark, where he was a male model. He began selling clothes as a traveling salesman, and while calling on Muse's Lady's Apparel in Atlanta, he met and fell in love with salesgirl Anne Cohen (1911–1986). Lemer established Herman Lemer Limited and sold clothing to southern and southwestern military post exchanges. The Lemers are shown preparing for an event at the Standard Club. (Davie Lemer Davis.)

BENJAMIN LEMER (1912–1984). Ben Lemer (Section 16, Block J-6) was captured by the Germans at the Battle of the Bulge during World War II and held as a POW in Germany's Stalag XIII. Following the war, he came to Atlanta to stay with his brother Herman. Ben married war widow Marjorie Hirsch Hess (1919–1984), whose husband, Bucky, had been shot down. From left to right are Marjorie Lemer, Ben Lemer, and sister-in-law Anne Lemer. (Davie Lemer Davis.)

H. Edward Cohen (d. 1938), Davie Bach Cohen (1876–1917). H. Edward Cohen (Section 16, J-3) left his hometown of Sandersville to prove to his businessman father that he could make it on his own in Atlanta. Cohen worked for Union Box Company as vice president and general manager. Among the company's many products were wooden boxes and crates. Family lore maintains that the company made the transport crates for the Coca-Cola Company. Edward married Davie Bach (1876–1917), who was a schoolteacher at the time. The couple had three children, but Edward was widowed in 1917 when Davie died while undergoing gallbladder surgery. Cohen was a member of the Temple, the Standard Club, and the Masonic lodge. (Both, Davie Lemer Davis.)

JACOB ELSAS (1842–1932). A German immigrant and Union army veteran, Jacob Elsas (Section 17, Block 278) came to Atlanta to work in dry goods. He was already running three businesses when he joined forces with fellow immigrant Isaac May. In 1872, they established Elsas, May and Company to manufacturer paper bags and cloth. Their mill became known as the Fulton Spinning Company. The area known as Cabbagetown was built to help house some of the factory's more than 100 workers. (Janice McDonald.)

ISAAC SINKOVITZ (1864–1937). Isaac Sinkovitz (Section 16, J5) left his native Russia, ultimately settling in Atlanta to sell dry goods and groceries. But by 1905, he had a new business—a saloon. The Jewish community was known for its own temperance, so those managing bars had reputations for managing legitimate establishments. Sinkovitz was one of several Russian Jewish immigrants who were proprietors of bars on Decatur Street. (Janice McDonald.)

Henry Aaron Alexander (1874–1967). A prominent attorney, scholar, and religious leader, Hank Alexander (Section 18, Block 359) is best known for his founding of the Atlanta Historical Society (now the Atlanta History Center). He also served as its president for many years. Alexander was Leo Frank's defense attorney during his murder trial. He and prosecutor Hugh Dorsey were classmates and friends at the University of Georgia and found themselves on opposing sides. Alexander served as a captain in World War I before returning to his law practice. He was also a member of the Georgia House of Representatives. Just as the Great Depression was hitting, Alexander built what was the largest home on Peachtree Road at the time. It had 15,000 square feet, 33 rooms, and 13 bathrooms. Pictured are Hugh Dorsey (left) and Hank Alexander. (Breman Museum.)

LUCILLE SELIG FRANK (1883–1957), EMILE SELIG (1949–1914), JOSEPHINE COHEN SELIG (1862–1920). The ashes of Lucille Frank (above) are buried in an unmarked spot between the graves of her parents, Emile and Josephine Selig (Block 279, Lot 58). In 1910, the prominent couple arranged for their daughter to marry New Yorker Leo Frank, a supervisor of his uncle's National Pencil Factory. In an anti-Semitic charged atmosphere, Frank was accused in 1913 of murdering a teenaged factory worker named Mary Phagan. His trial drew national attention, and he was found guilty despite evidence to the contrary. When Gov. John Slaton commuted his death sentence to life in prison, a group of vigilantes broke into Frank's jail and lynched him. Lucille never remarried, instead choosing to lead a quiet life away from the public eye, working at Rich's Department store in the glove department. (Leo Frank Organization.)

ANDRE (ENDRE) STEINER (1908–2009). Born in Austria-Hungary (present-day Slovakia), Andre (Endre) Steiner (Section 16, Block J9) was arrested by Nazis in World War II, only to be freed and forced to work on their projects. He used his influence to help better conditions for Jews in prison camps as well as offering bribes to spare many from death. With the changing face of his homeland after the war, he moved to the United States, then Cuba, before returning to settle in Atlanta, where he had relatives. His architectural skills garnered international acclaim. Steiner served as vice president of the Urban Design Department of the American Institute of Planners. As one of Atlanta's most celebrated architects, he designed numerous neighborhoods, most notably laying plans for Stone Mountain Park as well as the campus of Emory University, where he taught architectural design. (Brno Architecture Manual.)

Five
Confederate Memorial Grounds

The Lion of the Confederacy. Over 3,000 unknown Confederate soldiers lay at in the Confederate Memorial Grounds of Oakland. The Lion of the Confederacy statue serves as their headstone. Commemorated on April 26, 1894, the lion was commissioned by the Ladies Memorial Association. Sculptor T.M. Brady of Canton used the largest piece of marble quarried from North Georgia at that time. His paws wrapped around the Confederate battle flag, the lion lies mortally wounded. (HOF.)

Brig. Gen. Alfred Iverson (1829–1911). For all his victories in battle, Brig. Gen. Alfred Iverson (Section K, Grave 4) is best known for the disastrous ambush of his troops at Gettysburg. He lost more than 500 men, and two battalions surrendered. Iverson first enrolled in the Tuskegee Military Institute in Alabama at age 17 during the Mexican War. When the Civil War began, he resigned his position as lieutenant in the US Army to become a captain in the 20th North Carolina Cavalry Regiment. He was severely wounded at the Battle of Gaines Mill and recovered to join the Army of Northern Virginia. After the Battle of Antietam, he was promoted to brigadier general. Following the Gettysburg catastrophe, he was reassigned back to Georgia, where his brigade defeated troops under Maj. Gen. George Stoneman near Macon. Iverson is depicted below at the prison stockade in Florence, South Carolina. (Both, LOC.)

GEN. CLEMENT EVANS (1833–1911). Gen. Clement Evans (Section K, Grave 9) resigned from the Georgia Legislature to join the Confederate Army as a private. Rising quickly, he achieved the rank of general, fighting in every major battle of the Civil War in Northern Virginia. Evans was wounded five times (twice severely). He commanded the 31st Georgia Infantry (Bartow Guards), which made it farther north than any other Confederate unit, reaching York, Pennsylvania, in the Gettysburg campaign. His was the last unit to leave Union territory following the end of the war. Evans made a promise to God that he would enter the ministry and did so, ministering various churches for 28 years. Active among Confederate veterans, he helped organize the United Confederate Veterans. His body lay in state in the Georgia capitol rotunda following his death. Evans County was named in his honor. (LOC.)

MAJ. GEN. JOHN BROWN GORDON (1832–1904). Maj. Gen. John B. Gordon (Section K, Grave 4) was one of Robert E. Lee's most trusted and successful generals. Before the war, he was a planter, attorney, and businessman, investing in coal mines in Georgia and Tennessee. He became captain of a mountaineer company known as the "Raccoon Roughs," which, once the war started, was incorporated into the 6th Alabama Regiment. Gordon earned respect at the Battle of Manassas and was wounded severely several times during the course of the war. Postwar, Gordon was elected first as state senator, then Georgia governor (twice), and ultimately US senator. He was the first president of the United Confederate Veterans. His wife, Fanny Gordon, is buried beside him. (Left, LOC; below, Janice McDonald.)

GERALD ARASTUS SEYMOUR (1846–1937). G.A. Seymour (Section E 1-1) was the final person laid to rest in the Confederate Memorial Grounds, 73 years after the final wartime interment. Born in Lumpkin, Georgia, Seymour served as a private in the Georgia Volunteer Infantry for the Army of Tennessee. His division was known as "the Wards." He moved to Atlanta and worked as a traveling salesman for the Armour Fertilizer Company. (Janice McDonald.)

PVT. BRYANT GOODWIN (D. 1862). Bryant Goodwin (B-10) hailed from Arkansas and when he enlisted in the 8th Infantry in April 1863. The company was originally designated as "G," also known as the "Lawrence Dead Shots," with Capt. Joseph C. Holmes. The unit was originally organized as Company H in Pawhaten, Arkansas, in Lawrence County, on April 4, 1864. On May 10, the company's designation was changed to Company G. Private Goodwin passed away four days later. (Janice McDonald.)

James M. Hambright (1843–1863). James M. Hambright (A-16-24) was part of the Palmetto Sharpshooters Regiment, which was organized in April 1862 in South Carolina. Hambright's company was known as the Jasper Light Infantry from the York District. The brigade was en route to Virginia in September 1863 and changed trains in Atlanta. It is unclear what happened to Hambright, but he was hospitalized in the Institute Hospital, where he died. (Janice McDonald.)

Lucien Braham Weakley (1835–1863). One of the magnolia trees in Oakland stands behind the headstone of Tennessee-born Pvt. Lucien Weakley (A-12-43). Weakley had been married only three months to Adeline Bradley (1840–1908) when he was shot in the knee during the Battle of Chickamauga. Brought to Atlanta's Soldier's Hospital, he died of his injuries. His brother planted a magnolia sprout at his grave soon after his death. His widow never remarried. (Janice McDonald.)

WILLIAM ANDERSON MCCARTY (1825–1863).
William McCarty (B-4-7) was a planter in Talladega, Alabama, when he enlisted in the Confederate army in 1861. He left his wife of six years behind and headed off to war. As part of the 8th Alabama Regiment, he was involved in the Battle of Chickamauga. He was wounded September 21 and sent to Atlanta's Gate City Hospital, where he died two weeks later. McCarty actually has two headstones. One resembles the other military markers at Oakland, and this one, which is much larger, gives details of his death. (Janice McDonald.)

LT. ROBERT CASON STEWART (1830–1863).
The tombstone of Lt. Robert Stewart (C-3-9) reads, "A loving husband, a father, dear, a faithful soldier, is buried here." Stewart was a young father of three from Winston County when he joined the 5th Mississippi Regiment and was wounded in the Battle of Murfreesboro, Tennessee. He died at Atlanta's Fairground Hospital. Another headstone for Stewart can be found in Good Hope Cemetery in Fern Springs, Mississippi, where his wife, Virginia, is buried. (Janice McDonald.)

Pvt. William Daniel Prescott Jr. (1829–1863). Pvt. William Prescott Jr. (Section H) grew up in Coffee County, Alabama, farming and helping run his father's sugarcane mill. He was married to Elizabeth Bodifeld and had two children when he joined Company K of the Alabama Volunteers. He died from battle injuries at the Atlanta Medical College. His brother James Hiram was killed in 1862 near Tupelo, Mississippi. Brother John Wesley Prescott died in battle at New Hope Church, Alabama. (Janice McDonald.)

Pvt. Steven Harrison Wilkes (1845–1863). S.H. Wilkes (Section H) grew up in South Georgia and was just 17 years old when he enlisted in the 5th Regiment of the Georgia Infantry. His father, Isaac, was a member of the Georgia Militia. Harrison eventually moved to Company A of the 2nd Battalion Georgia Sharpshooters. He was serving with them during the Battle of Missionary Ridge in Tennessee, where he was critically wounded and died from his injuries. (Janice McDonald.)

Six
EAST HILL

LAURA ISABELL "LOLLIE BELLE" MOORE WYLIE (1858–1923). Lollie Belle Wylie (Section 17, Block 282) made a name for herself as a journalist, composer, and author. She championed other writers as well. Her first book of verses, *The Legend of Cherokee Rose*, was published in 1887, the same year her husband, Hartsfield "Hart" Wylie (1855–1887), died. Suddenly, she was a single mom and the breadwinner. Her song "Georgia" was the state's official song for more than 55 years. (*American Women.*)

Gottfried Leonard Norrman (1848–1909). Swedish-born G.L. Norrman (Section 22, Block 317) had studied architecture extensively throughout Scandinavia and Germany before settling in Atlanta. Over the next almost three decades, he used changing technology to help design iconic buildings across the South, such as the stunning Queen Anne–style Ivy Hall (shown here) for the Edward Peters family, the castle-like Windsor Hotel in Americus, and the Savannah Citizens Bank Building. Atlanta's three Cotton States Expositions featured his work. Norrman helped found the Southern Chapter of the American Institute of Architects. He was known for his popularity among the social set, so it came as a shock when one evening after a seemingly normal card game, he returned to his room at the new Candler Building and committed suicide. (Both, AHC.)

ZACHARIAH H. SMITH (1833–1906). Zach Smith (Section 17, Block 369) was an early settler in Atlanta, serving on the city's first police board as well as nine years on the water board. The city directory lists his occupation as a carpenter. For 18 years, he worked as a master car builder for the Richmond and Danville Railroad. The gravestones for Smith and his wife, Euphenia (1843–1920), simply state their first names. (Janice McDonald.)

ANNIE FARREN HERLEY TUCKER (1850–1909). Annie Tucker (Section 17, Block 296) was a young mother with three small children when her husband, attorney John Thomas Herley (1837–1880), passed away. When she married Dr. Thomas W. Tucker (1850–1890), her two daughters took his last name, while John Jr. maintained his father's name. That union was short as well. Dr. Tucker died just shy of his 40th birthday. (Janice McDonald.)

BERNARD MALLON (1824–1879). The Irish-born Bernard Mallon (Section 17, Block 291) made a lasting impact on education in Atlanta as well as in Texas. Having served as a teacher and then superintendent of Atlanta's schools, he was known as someone who devoted his life to education. He died in Texas just 11 days after establishing the Sam Houston Normal Institute, which was designed to help professionally train teachers. The day of his funeral back in Atlanta, school was suspended for so that the board of education, principals, teachers, and even students could attend his services. His Oakland monument was erected by teachers and students and declares, "Patient and Wise Teacher, he loved God and Little Children." (Left, Sam Houston State University; below, Janice McDonald.)

Dr. Gustav Garnett Roy (1836–1901). Dr. G.G. Roy (Section 17, Block 293) graduated from medical school in his native Virginia but joined the Confederate army during the war. He eventually became assistant surgeon in the Confederate army, overseeing hospitals in Atlanta as well as the Federal prison in Andersonville. He helped organize the Southern Medical College in Atlanta. Roy was also elected councilman to the Sixth Ward for two terms. (*Memoirs of Georgia*.)

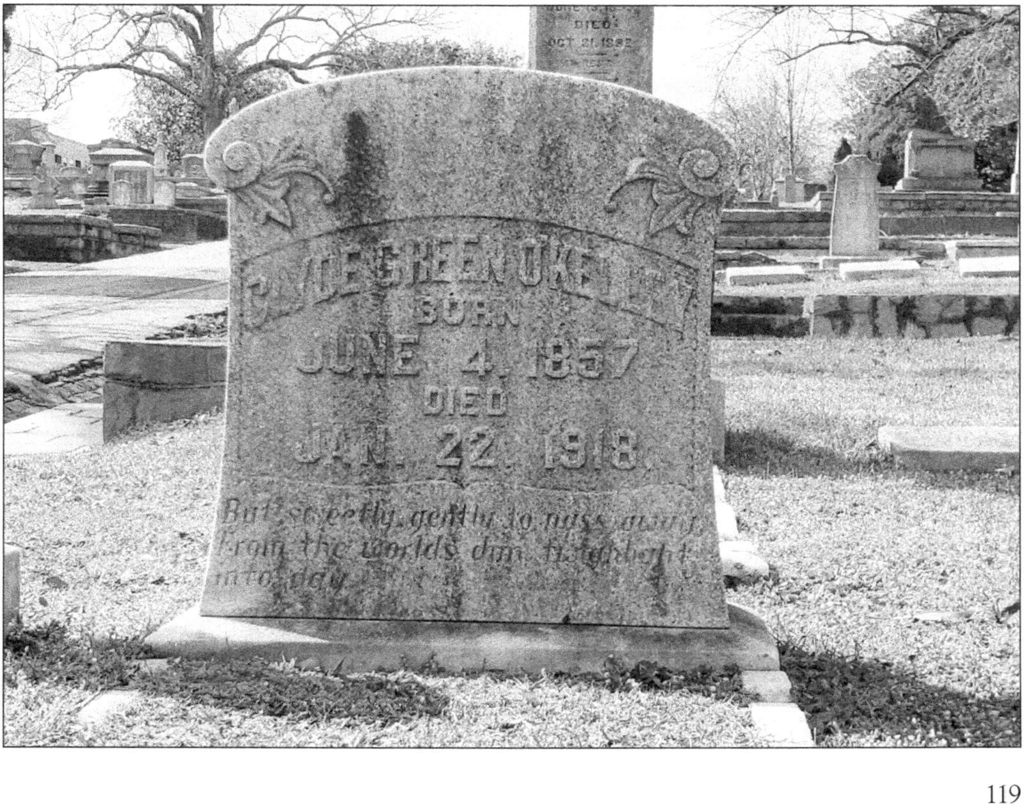

Clyde Bloodworth Barrett Green O'Kelley (1857–1918). Two of the three husbands of Clyde O'Kelley (Section 22, Block 409) are buried near her. George G. Barrett (1853–1993) died while working at the Southern Express Railroad Company. Five years later, she married Dr. Elijah Washington Green (1859–1892). Upon his death, Atlanta newspapers declared Green was idolized by friends and "no citizen was more deserved to be esteemed." The twice-widowed Green next married widower and postmaster Dean O'Kelley (1856–1921). O'Kelley is buried in Rockdale County. (Janice McDonald.)

LOUISE RICHARDSON ALLEN (1917–2008). Even before becoming first lady of Atlanta, Louise Allen (Section 17, Block 296) was making herself known in the city. As part of one of the city's oldest families (Inman), she was involved in numerous civic organizations before marrying Ivan Allen Jr. (1911–2003). Among her many accomplishments, Allen was a founder of the Atlanta Speech School, president of the Atlanta Junior League, and a trustee of the Westminster Schools, Henrietta Egleston Hospital (now part of Children's Healthcare of Atlanta), the Georgia Trust Foundation, the Cherokee Garden Club, and the Historic Oakland Foundation. Her husband served two terms as Atlanta's mayor, from 1962 to 1970. The 1942 photograph above shows her over his shoulder, to the left, and center at a World War II deployment dinner. The photograph below shows her gardening at her Buckhead home in 1961. (Both, AHC.)

REV. HENRY MILTON QUILLIAN (1851–1931). The Quillians came from a long line of Methodist ministers who settled in North Georgia. Rev. Henry Quillian (Section 23, Block 397) was the son and the grandson of a preacher. He maintained the family tradition by joining the ministry. Henry served on the North Georgia Methodist Conference for 53 years. As city alderman, his brother Fletcher Arnold Quillian (1859–1928) was still involved in the church but was more active in politics. Fletcher was on the Atlanta City Council that voted in 1908 to expand the city limits. He also worked to try and secure bonds for improvement of the Atlanta city sewer systems. In 1915, Fletcher ran for mayor but lost to Asa Candler. Pictured from left to right are brothers Fletcher, Rev. Joseph Asbury Quillian, Henry, and James Tarpley Quillian. (Above, Fredric Martin; below, Janice McDonald.)

Edward Hamilton Inman (1881–1931), Emily MacDougald Inman (1881–1965). Edward (left) and Emily Inman (Section 17, Block 272) left perhaps their greatest legacy in Swan House, considered one of Atlanta's most iconic homes. The Princeton-educated Edward was part of one of Atlanta's oldest and richest families. Their fortune was largely built on cotton, railroads, and real estate. When their home in Ansley Park burned, the Inmans commissioned famed architect Phillip Trammel Shutze to design a home for them in Buckhead. Its name is due to the swan motif throughout. Edward passed away just three years after they moved in. Emily lived there until her death in 1965; she arranged for the house and its 20-acre property to be donated to the neighboring Atlanta History Center. (Left, AHC; below, Janice McDonald.)

BRIG. GEN. WILLIAM STEPHEN WALKER (1822–1899). Harvard-educated Brig. Gen. William S. Walker (Section 22, Block 319) had served with distinction in the Mexican War. He resigned his position at captain in the US Army to join the Confederacy. Walker spent the early part of the Civil War behind a desk, doing administrative duties. During his first battle in May 1864, Walker's right leg was shattered when his horse was shot and killed during fighting with South Carolina forces behind enemy lines near Richmond. Walker's foot was amputated, and he was held as a prisoner of war. After he was freed in a prisoner exchange, he took a command in North Carolina. Postwar, he settled in Atlanta. (LOC.)

JOHN MCNAMARA (1833–1907), ANNIE MCNAMARA (1838–1891). The McNamaras hailed from County Mayo in Ireland. John and Annie McNamara (Section 16, Block 346) also had a son, John (1862–1881), who was listed as an "Irish horse trader." The McNamaras were believed to be part of a tradition among eight families where they would travel as a group with a covered wagon offering livery service and trading horses. Atlanta was a favorite location for burials because Catholic priests were available. (Janice McDonald.)

GOV. MICHAEL HOKE SMITH (1855–1931). Hoke Smith (Section 21, Block 303) was a trial attorney and education proponent when, in 1887, he purchased the *Atlanta Journal* and used it as a platform to enter politics as a Democrat. Despite his being labeled a Progressive, his governorship was marred by efforts to disenfranchise blacks, sparking race riots. While still serving as governor, Smith was appointed to fill a vacant US Senate seat and continued to hold both offices despite objections. (LOC.)

BENJAMIN HARVEY HILL (1823–1882). Ben Hill (section 22, Block 315) is considered one of the great orators of the 1800s and held both state and national offices. He graduated from the University of Georgia and was practicing law when he was elected first to the Georgia House and then to the Georgia Senate. Despite opposing succession, Hill served as a Confederate senator representing Georgia in the Confederate Senate, for which he was later arrested and held for two months in New York's Fort Lafayette. He returned to Georgia to practice law and to oppose Republican Reconstruction. Hill was elected to the US House of Representatives for the Ninth Congressional District, and served until he was elected to the US Senate. Ben Hill County is named for him. (LOC.)

Frederick Augustus Hickson (1857–1916). F.A. Hickson (Section 23, Block 399) arrived at Little Bighorn immediately following Custer's Last Stand and witnessed the horrible aftermath of battle. The Canada native also met legendary showman William Frederick "Buffalo Bill" Cody. Hickson performed briefly in Cody's Wild West show before making a name for himself as an inventor and entrepreneur. He held several patents and helped build the first streetcar lines in Atlanta and Macon. (LOC.)

Julius Astor Fischer (1857–1934). Considered one of Atlanta's pioneers, Julius Fischer (Section 23, Block 397) was a successful merchant and building contractor. His company helped build some of the finest homes in Atlanta, including his own at the edge of the newly developed Grant Park. Fischer was active in city government, serving on the city water board. (HOF.)

POTTER'S FIELD. Potter's Field covers seven and a half acres in the northeastern section of Oakland Cemetery's 48 acres. There are an estimated 7,500 people who rest in unmarked graves beneath the quiet expanse of grass and granite. Prone to flooding, this was the least desirable of all the property at Oakland, so plots were not sold here. Some graves are less than a foot apart. Among those buried here are the unknown and unclaimed as well as some moderate-to-low-income individuals. Families who could not afford a plot could choose to be buried in this area of Oakland with their graves unmarked. In the 1970s, archaeological studies by Georgia State University found numerous graves that appeared to have had some sort of attempt at marking that had likely disappeared over time. The last burials in Potter's Field were in the 1880s. (Janice McDonald.)

Visit us at
arcadiapublishing.com